A GiFT FOR:

_____

FROM:

_____

HOW TO MAKE A MOOSE RUN

AND OTHER GREAT LESSONS MY DAD TAUGHT ME ABOUT LIFE AND FAITH

by
Gary Stanley

RIVER OAK PUBLISHING

Hallmark GIFT BOOKS

BOK 5040

How to Make a Moose Run
And Other Great Lessons My Dad Taught Me About Life and Faith
ISBN 1-68919-976-6
Copyright © 2001 by Gary Stanley

This edition published in 2001 by RiverOak Publishing,
exclusively for Hallmark Cards, Inc.

www.hallmark.com

DEDICATION

To my dad,
the man who taught me to see
with my heart—
and my other very present Dad
who is teaching me to live next to His heart.

Fathers interpret life for their children—
give life structure and meaning.
They do so whether they mean to or not.
It either becomes the foundation
on which we build a life,
or the rubble we dig out from under.

CONTENTS

SECTiON V, You Don't Have to Survive in Order to Succeed

SECTiON Vi, You Don't Have To Be Perfect for My World To Be Whole

SECTiON Vii, You Don't Have To Be Religious to Enjoy God

ACKNOWLEDGMENTS

There are a lot of folks to thank in a book that spans more than fifty years.

Mom, thank you for helping to keep alive my memories of Dad— the long talks, the photo albums. You treasured the keepsakes that could easily have disappeared. Thank you. Aunt Gloria, thank you for sharing your memories of growing up as Dad's little sister. Alma Dell, every family needs a family historian—thank you for taking on that role in our family. So few bother to remember, but you do.

John Kriz, you encouraged me to pursue in words what God was doing in my heart. Thank you. Ann Bowman, thank you for patiently battling for me to see how hurt and blessed I truly am. Mike Constantz, thank you for acknowledging the call on my life to write and encouraging me in that direction. Dudley Delffs, thank you for your wise counsel on how to organize the chapters; I was stuck.

Mark Gilroy, thanks for believing in me as a writer and making a place for me at RiverOak Publishing. Debbie Justus, thank you for crafting the shape of this book and striving to gain it a wider audience. Shawna McMurry, thank you for shepherding my labor of love into print. Dear Barbara Scott, your encouragement and edit of my words have been a calming and challenging hand on my heart— still wonder if you're not an angel in disguise.

Janet, I still remember the first time we met and you pulled out your red pen to edit my clumsy words. Thank you for being my friend, for believing in me and navigating me through the wild, wonderful world of publishing. Kirsten, thank you for pursuing chapter inserts and quotes with me. Who would have ever guessed the true history of the Whoopee Cushion if not for you! Cliff and Marsha, thank you for sharing yourselves and giving me the ideas for several chapter inserts, we love being your neighbors again. Phil Chorlian, I love your take on what it truly means to be holy; your friendship couldn't have come at a better time. Thank you.

Luci, you saw what I couldn't and as a result this is a far better book than would have been written. You call me to a level of intimacy and courage I only dreamed of. Your name isn't on the cover, but it is in my heart for always.

iNTRODUCTiON

G. L. Stanley was a big man. He had big hands, a big nose, and a big heart. His black wavy hair ended in a slight widow's peak above steel-gray eyes. His thin lips and smallish chin promised a dimple that never quite materialized. He was one of those people who always seemed on the brink of sharing some wonderful secret that would make everything all right.

Those who kept company with him laughed more than they would have otherwise. They felt safe in his presence. They let down their guard and pretense and discovered that there was more to life than meets the eye.

He was the most remarkable man I've ever known. He interpreted life for me. He was my dad.

It takes years to discover who you really are—what is yours and what is just on loan from your parents. Lessons planted in childhood don't always grow with the man. I lost much of what my father taught me after he was gone, and it's taken a long time to get some of it back. Fortunately, the journey and memories have been filled with more than a few belly laughs, embarrassing moments that are no longer all that embarrassing, manly deeds, cowardly acts, and a few tears.

Dad died in his forty-eighth year. I had just turned thirteen.

Some will read these stories and think that I have idealized my dad. They are right. In some important ways, Dad has remained who he was in the memory of my adolescence. Others will wonder if the stories are true. They are.

Memory plays tricks on all of us. I am no exception. And time embellishes every story to some extent. But I have taken great pains to tell as much of the truth as I could remember. Of equal importance for me, the stories are finally sorting themselves out in a meaningful way; I have found a better place to put my longings for a dad.

My hope is that you will try on these stories and find that they fit an old memory of your own or help you plant a new memory. Perhaps they can serve as a guide and encouragement to you as you live out the stories your children will remember long after you're gone. And maybe—just maybe—you too will learn some unexpected lessons from the very present Father of us all.

IF WE'RE NOT HAVING FUN, WE MUST BE DOING SOMETHING WRONG

SECTION I

HEALING HUMOR

Laughter is not only good for your soul, it is good for your body. Study after study shows laughter's healing qualities. A good laugh can help you think more clearly, engage life more creatively, and solve problems more productively. Humor has been shown to improve your immune system by increasing antibodies, aid your digestion, and increase the blood flow to every major organ in your body.

We human beings were created for laughter—it burns calories, reduces fatigue, exercises the heart, and suppresses the hormones that induce stress. Embracing the funny side of life just makes you feel good, and that's not bad.[1]

HOW TO MAKE A MOOSE RUN

nless you're trying to carry a tune, I figure a good whistle is about one thing—volume—an ear-splitting, glass-breaking, through-the-teeth, taxi-alerting kind of whistle. I've had a dozen gifted whistlers attempt to teach me how to make this shrill whistle. They have all failed. It remains one of life's great mysteries to me.

Not possessing a shrill whistle has been a severe handicap in my audible range of expression, but I've learned to adapt with a modicum of grace and civility. (Still think it's cruelly unfair that some can, and I can't!) However, I can whistle at normal volume. In fact, I know four ways of doing that. Dad taught me three, and the other one I picked up from my long-time buddy, Mike.

I can pucker my lips and whistle out and in. (That's two ways.) Mike taught me to roll my tongue lengthwise and blow across it much the way you do a pop bottle to get a foghorn sound—took me years to perfect that one.

The fourth way is my dad's patented "moose call." It's a bit more complicated to explain. Basically, you cup both hands together to make an air pocket such that your two thumbs can bend to cover the only opening. It's important there be just one opening and no leaks or else it won't work—trust me. Put your upper lip over both bent thumb knuckles and blow straight down. If you're really good, you can slightly open one hand and get a two-pitch sound reminiscent of a tugboat whistle.

Dad and I called moose all the time from our front yard, at football games, on camping trips, and any other place where a good stout whistle was appropriate. Never saw a single moose for all that blowing.

Then the summer of my eighth year, we took a family vacation to Yellowstone National Park—Old Faithful, a massive visitors' lodge made of giant timbers and crossbeams, begging bears aplenty, my first earthquake, and a herd of moose!

A dozen moose were grazing in a meadow about a hundred yards back from the road. Between the moose and us was a seven- or eight-foot-high barbed wire fence. It was one of those no-nonsense fences strung tight with vertical wire woven between the horizontal strands to keep them together.

Dad pulled the car over, and I jumped out to try out my moose call. I positioned my hands just right and blew long and clear—even added the two-pitched trick for good measure. Not one of the moose moved. Didn't even look up between chews.

Dad put his arm around me and said, "Want to see those moose run? Maybe they won't come when we call, but I bet we can make them run." With that, he started to work his way over the barbed-wire fence. I squeezed between the bottom two wires. That fence was strung so tight there wasn't any give in it at all. It took us the better part of five minutes to get across without getting cut, stuck, or poked.

Once on the other side, we started to walk toward the herd. Dad waved his arms and hollered, and I continued to work my moose call. We marched forward like a couple of crazy tourists. The herd of moose continued to ignore us in favor of munching the meadow. They'd probably seen it all before. We continued forward, waving, hollering, and whistling.

Then Dad picked up a pebble and flipped it in the general direction of the moose. That got their attention. The biggest moose in the herd finally looked up. He had a massive set of antlers and

LITTLE KNOWN MOOSE FACTS

Around 1700, the Swedish cavalry experimented with moose as "combat vehicles." The animals have better stamina and terrain mobility than horses and were expected to terrify enemy forces who probably had never seen a moose. They were good animals to ride and could be trained just as well as horses in all respects but for one: the moose is a smart animal, and the trainers could never get them to quit running away from artillery, muskets, pikes, and other weaponry.[2]

looked to be nearly seven feet tall. Probably tipped the scales at more than a thousand pounds. He picked up hooves the size of hubcaps and began to move. It was an amazing thing to watch—all that bulk picking up steam. It was all the more fascinating because he was moving in our direction. Still a good eighty yards from us, he was already too close for comfort!

"Run!" Dad hollered.

We put on a good show for the moose as we turned tail and scrambled for the fence. I suspect we turned in several personal bests that day—a new record for the twenty-yard dash, Dad's two-step fence climb, and my belly-flop wiggle under the wire. It's amazing what you can do when an angry moose is involved.

We caught our breath, hugged Mom, and got back in the car. For the next twenty miles, our conversation bounced back and forth between our foolishness, a growing respect for God's larger creatures, and our own miraculous escape. A few miles down the road, it occurred to Dad that we undoubtedly possessed the best moose call in the world: one that doesn't work!

WHAT MY DAD TAUGHT ME
Wisdom knows when to abandon one plan in favor of a better one.

> *A clever man commits no minor blunders.*
> —Johann Wolfgang von Goethe

THANKSGiViNG AND THE WHOOPEE CUSHiON

When Dad laughed, he laughed with his whole body, holding nothing back. He laughed so hard he sometimes cried. Laughter came easy and often to Dad. And there was a pretty good chance he was the instigator of whatever humorous bit of mischief happened to trigger his funny bone.

My dad was not above store-bought pranks, like a hand buzzer or the little red ball he would place between the porcelain and bottom of the toilet seat that squirted water on whomever happened to sit on it. Childish? Absolutely! Funny? Probably depended on which side of the bathroom door you happened to be on. Sensitive? Caring? Hardly. I think it had more to do with his love for gadgets than anything else.

Of course, he got as much as he gave. Practical jokes, shaggy-dog stories, and elaborate pranks were the norm in our home. But one incident stands head and shoulders above the rest.

In my early years, we spent every other Thanksgiving in Shamrock, Texas, at Mammuddy's and Pop Pop's. My grandparents' oak dining-room table, with its claw feet and multiple extensions, was stretched to its limits to accommodate all of the family. Everyone brought their favorite side dishes, and Mammuddy oversaw the cooking of an enormous turkey and the stuffing. She always added little chunks of liver to her stuffing, and no matter how diligent I was, a few of those foul-tasting things always ended up in my mouth. (I still have an aversion to liver in all forms.)

Preparing such a feast meant that we wouldn't sit down to dinner until well after the usual mealtime. Everything had to be just right, and everyone had to be seated before we could begin. There were two designated prayers for this meal: my grandfather, Pop Pop, and Uncle A. B. Now Pop Pop was a man of few words, and when it was his turn to deliver grace, it was short and sweet. Uncle A. B. was of the opposite ilk. His prayers were long, arduous, and all-inclusive. By the time he wound up one of his marathon prayers, half the stomachs at the table were growling, "Amen."

One year Dad knew it was Uncle A. B.'s turn to pray and thought this somber occasion could use a little levity. He'd brought a brand-new whoopee cushion he was dying to try out, and he was curious what effect it might have on this year's prayer. Together we hid the cushion under the chair pad at the head of the table and waited.

Everyone took their seats, including Uncle A. B., but nothing happened. Not so much as one tiny toot leaked from Dad's whoopee cushion. Go figure. The instructions for the device were pretty simple, but obviously something had been missed.

Uncle A. B. cleared his throat in preparation for one of his patented invocations as everyone bowed their heads and rested elbows on the table in anticipation of a good five to ten minutes worth of supplications and thanks. A. B. had just started to pray when he, too, leaned forward into a more penitent position. Apparently, when he had sat down, he had pinched shut the mouth of the whoopee cushion. However, with his shift of weight, the whoopee cushion began to do what it was created to do.

A series of sputtering, flatulent sounds began to accompany Uncle A. B.'s prayer. The rude noise was muffled yet distinct. The timing could hardly have been better—or worse, depending on your perspective. But what was one to do? Dad buried his head in his hands. Grinning sheepishly, I sneaked a peek to see everyone's reaction—a smile here, a frown there, the shake of a head, and the wrinkle of more than one nose.

Uncle A. B., determined to block out the distractions of the world, began to shift his weight as he dove deeper into his prayer. There was no way to tell when the whoopee cushion would be aroused and accompany another part of his prayer.

Dad tried his best to hold in the humor of the moment. His whole body shook. His nose ran. He cried. It was all he could do to keep from throwing his head back and laughing to the heavens.

A. B. and the whoopee cushion proved faithful to the end, each vying for attention. Dad could hardly breathe by the time it was all over. It was definitely not the most sacred moment on record.

As everyone looked up after the unusual pre-dinner duet, Dad began to wipe his eyes and dab his nose with his napkin. No one else at the table was quite sure what interpretation to put on what had just happened. Some probably thought it an unfortunate event best ignored. Others were likely struggling to regain their appetites.

THE GUILLOTINE AND THE WOODEE CUSHION

French chemist Antoine Laurent Lavoisier is famous for three things; one can't help but wonder if each didn't lead to the next.

First, as one of the pioneers of modern chemistry, he was credited with the discovery of oxygen's role in combustion. Second, Antoine was the inventor of a slightly different form of gaseous combustion—the whoopee cushion. And third, the French Revolution found him a worthy subject for the guillotine due, in all probability, to his aristocratic (and not so aristocratic) pursuits.[3]

However, Mammuddy was so deep into her own prayers that she failed to notice a single note of the errant song. She looked at her only son and surmised that G. L. had been deeply moved by Uncle A. B.'s prayer. She leaned over and patted his hand as she expressed her own sense of deep emotion and thankfulness over her family all being around her table. Dad was on the verge of pulling a stomach muscle.

The physical manifestation of emotion can easily be misunderstood. The difference between pain and pleasure is far smaller than one might suspect. And it is often the source of one's physical response rather than the response itself that determines the comedy or contrition of the moment. Dad hid his face in his napkin and just nodded as his body was obviously racked with some emotion.

I don't think Grandmother ever found out that a whoopee cushion had joined the family's Thanksgiving meal that year. But I don't remember ever seeing it again. For all I know, it found its final resting place there under the cushion of the chair at the head of the table. If Mammuddy ever found it, she probably would have concluded it was a fancy hot-water bottle or something; she usually saw the best in whatever or whomever was at hand, including her prankster son.

WHAT MY DAD TAUGHT ME

Sometimes it's better to let folks draw their own conclusions.

> *Imagination was given to man to compensate him for what he is not, and a sense of humor was provided to console him for what he is.*
>
> —Robert Walpole (*my many times great-grandfather*)

HoW NoT To EAT A TooTSiE RoLL PoP

i have long enjoyed the entertainment value of food, especially what you can do with it in your mouth (drives my wife crazy). I know how to twist the top off an Oreo cookie, leaving the cream center entirely on one half for licking, and then dig a hole in the creamless half with my lower front teeth without cracking the edges. I've been known to hold a peanut M&M in my mouth, letting the entire candy-coated outer shell and milk chocolate melt away, before crunching into the peanut. And I can shell a mouthful of sunflower seeds and spit out the husks while holding all of the seeds in one cheek so that I can enjoy all of them at once.

It is a sad thing to my way of thinking that Takola Sticks are all but gone. There are few candies that were so much fun to eat. That colored wax tube was filled with flavored liquid ready to burst into your mouth (or down the front of your shirt if you weren't careful) when you bit into it. Then you got to chew the wax until all the flavor was gone and bits of it stuck to your teeth.

However, despite my prowess in the arena of mouth gymnastics, I was almost done in by a Tootsie Roll Pop. We were on our way to another week-long, spaghetti-filled visit with Little Red (a.k.a. Aunt Gertrude). Dad was driving down the familiar two-lane road between Fort Worth and Palestine, the headlights illuminating the blacktop.

Sitting in the backseat with nothing to do, I unwrapped a chocolate-flavored Tootsie Roll Pop and immersed myself in one of my favorite pastimes. A Tootsie Roll Pop can last a long time if you resist the urge to crunch down on the candied outer layer. You can hold it between your cheek and gum like a wad of chewing gum and let the juices trickle down the back of your throat. It is also ideally suited to test the various taste sensors that reside in your mouth. Believe it or not, a Tootsie Roll tastes different under your tongue than it does on the top of your tongue. And the front part of the tongue savors candy in a distinctly different way than the back part of the tongue.

I was experimenting with the taste sensations to be had from the roof of my mouth when I accidentally slid the Tootsie Roll a bit too far back in my throat. The gag reflex took over, and I swallowed the whole thing—cardboard stick and all.

My interest in taste sensations quickly gave way to my interest in breathing. I coughed and sputtered and tried to reach the cardboard stick of the offending candy stuck halfway down my throat, all to no avail. Dad looked over his shoulder at his retching son and quickly pulled over to the side of the road. He flung open the back door, plucked me out of the car, and hauled me around to the headlights to get a better look. Obviously, something was block-ing my air passage. His big fingers couldn't begin to navigate the small opening of a four-year-old's mouth, and time was running out.

I don't know what inspired him to do it; maybe it's written in some life-saving man-ual, or maybe an angel whispered in his ear. In any event, Dad picked me up by my heels and began to jerk me up and down, my head descending within inches of the pavement, only to be launched back up into the air by his strong arms. The third time

TOOTSIE ROLLS SAVE LIVES!

If you think anything that's been around as long as Tootsie Rolls (1896) has probably influenced history, you're right. In November 1950, the First Marine Division, along with some British commandos and South Korean policemen, were retreating through the Chang Jin Mountains before ten divisions of the Chinese Communist Army.

The subzero temperatures fouled everything from the artillery to the food. Without the means to heat their frozen rations, the men were close to starvation. However, they discovered boxes and boxes of frozen Tootsie Rolls among their supplies. The candy curbed their hunger, and the sugar gave them energy to successfully complete their retreat to safety.[4]

was a charm, and with the help of gravity, inertia, and probably an angel with small hands, the Tootsie Roll Pop plopped out onto the asphalt.

It all happened so quickly. I hardly had time to reflect on the fear that gripped me before I found myself in Daddy's arms, with Mom stroking my hair, and me gulping down gallons of night air. Saved!

There have been other times when my spirit was all but suffocated under my foolish experiments with flavors of life far less innocent than a Tootsie Roll Pop. Caught in the grip of fear, unable to breathe, I finally croak out some half-choked plea to the Daddy of daddies. And just like my dad, God is willing to take extreme measures to clear the blockage that is choking the life out of me.

WHAT MY DAD TAUGHT ME

Sometimes rough treatment is the kindest thing happening in the moment.

Sometimes we turn to God when our foundations are shaking only to find that it is God who is shaking them.

THE SCORPION AND THE STRIPTEASE

ur home on the outskirts of Fort Worth, Texas, was a "spec" house. In other words, Dad built it in hopes of selling it and using the profit to build the next one. Dad had no big backers for his subdivision and no large line of credit—just a dream. The house went on the market and was featured in the local newspaper and a couple of trade magazines, but there were no takers. Rather than let it sit and make double house payments, we moved in, reasoning that it might be easier for any would-be buyers to envision themselves in an already occupied home.

For a year Mom, Dad, and I lived there, way over our heads, on a shoestring, enjoying the digs. Dad eventually sold that house to our family doctor, Doyle Doss, who was also a family friend and Dad's deer-hunting buddy—probably the only person we knew who could have afforded that place.

Living in undeveloped parts of Texas means that you have to keep an eye out for snakes and other things that creep in the night—especially scorpions. Scorpions look like something right out of the lower regions of Hell. There's nothing inviting about a land shrimp with a stinger tail poised overhead. I'm pretty sure everyone who has ever seen one of those things up close and personal universally holds this opinion.

So when a scorpion was discovered in our house, the alarm went out and the designated bug killer went into action. Dad found an appropriate tool of destruction—a shovel with a long handle—and proceeded to pummel the beast into oblivion. Of course, where there is one scorpion, it's reasonable to assume there may be more. Dad instructed us to shake out our shoes before putting them on and to be on the lookout. Mostly it was common sense stuff, but a touch of paranoia lingered after that first invasion. A few nights later, the main event was to be played out.

Dad was already in bed when Mom appeared in the lighted doorway of the bathroom. She was wearing an elaborate silk bathrobe and pajama thing reminiscent of something from the Far East. As she drifted toward the bed, Dad noticed something out of place on her sleeve. Somehow a scorpion had managed to attach itself to

Mom's nightwear. With some alarm, Dad shouted his observation as he pointed out the beast.

Mom, already conditioned by several days of scorpion searches, reacted as if she'd just met the serious end of a cattle prod. She jumped and hollered and flailed her arms as she spun around.

"Where is it!" Mom screamed. Dad had no idea. The scorpion was no longer visible. Mom was soon so tangled up in her nightwear that the scorpion could have been anywhere.

Dad tried to help her out of her robe, but he might as well have tried to take the saddle off a bucking bronco. Finally he stepped back to size up the situation and his wife.

Now my dad was a kind man, a wonderful man, and an honest man. And he wouldn't have hurt my mom for the world or let anything happen to her. But Dad was also a man with a sense of humor and not one to miss an opportunity.

The scorpion appeared to have vanished into the great unknown, but Mom continued to dance around demanding to know where the little beast was. Dad pointed vaguely in her general direction in a gesture that meant the scorpion could be anywhere. Mom took this to mean that the scorpion was still attached to some bit of clothing. With a blur of motion, she shed her silk bathrobe. For some reason this struck Dad as funny, and he continued to point at various articles of clothing. Mom wasted no time setting a record for wiggling out of her pajamas and was soon jumping and whirling around in the same condition in which she entered the world.

AT FIRST BLUSH

L ife is full of embarrassing moments, and frantically jumping around in the nude ought to rank up there near the top. However, Mom's scorpion-induced striptease didn't result in so much as a blush—it didn't meet the conditions for embarrassment to occur. Experts in human behavior contend that four conditions must be present before we blush with embarrassment or self-mortification:

1. Some goof or failure must occur for which you feel some level of responsibility.

2. The potentially embarrassing event has to occur unexpectedly leaving no time to prepare.

3. The moment has to take place in public.

4. You have to care what others think about your goof.

Oh yes, it turns out that if you simply admit your embarrassment and carry on, you may actually be held in higher esteem than if nothing had happened at all.[5]

Of course I saw none of this and only learned of the scorpion and the striptease the next morning over breakfast. We never did find that scorpion, but that was not the end of the story.

A few days later, Dr. Doss and his wife were visiting, and in the recounting of the scorpion story, Dad innocently asked Doyle, "Have you ever tried to get the clothes off a hysterical woman?" Doyle paused in thought and then said, "No, not in a long time."

Oddest of all, it was Mom who enjoyed telling the tale over the years, not Dad.

WHAT MY DAD TAUGHT ME

The very thing that made you jump out of your skin last
night can be the basis of a good story the next morning.

*There aren't too many occasions,
outside of marriage, where you can get out
of trouble and your clothes at the same time.*

—Gary Stanley

THE DEER HUNTERS

Hunting with Daddy

Ever tried to take a little kid hunting? Little kids and hunting are like oil and water—they don't mix. Hunting requires stealth and patience, two commodities woefully lacking in most youngsters. Dad liked to hunt. But he liked to be with me more, so he took me with him.

I vaguely remember one hunting expedition. I was wearing the only bright red thing I owned—a plastic slicker with a hood. With every step I took, my raincoat crackled, swished, and popped. Of course, I knew how to move through the forest like a shadow, as silent as a ghost. I put my fingers in my ears and asked Dad every few feet, "I sure am being quiet, aren't I, Daddy?" If I couldn't hear anything, it stood to reason that none of the creatures we were stalking could hear either.

I don't think we saw hide nor hair of a deer that day, or any other wildlife for that matter. Naturally I heard about my strategy for keeping quiet on hunting trips at just about every family gathering for years!

Elk Mountain

When I was sixteen, I went through my Jeremiah Johnson phase. I decided to pack up my horse, Sam, and head for Elk Mountain for a few days of solitary camping and hunting—living off the land.

I've never been so cold in all my life! I don't think the temperature ever came close to the sunny side of zero. I soon gave up any hope of bagging an elk in favor of staying warm. I built a huge campfire, put on every stitch of clothing I had, wrapped up in my sleeping bag, and hunkered down next to the fire. Sam kept inching his way closer to the fire. I guess the fear of fire only goes so far when you're real cold. Sam got so close, he singed the hair on his belly and then stubbornly resisted me when I tried to push him away from the flames.

I began to wonder if the deer might feel the same as Sam did about the cold and cozy up to a nice warm fire. They don't. After a day and a half of breathing smoke and trying to stay warm, I finally gave up and went home.

The Nosy Deer

I'm not the only one who's made a fool of himself on a hunting trip. Whenever a campfire burned low and there was a lull in the conversation, it was a fair bet that

How to Make a Moose Run

SAMSON THE ELK

If you visit Estes Park, Colorado, and the surrounding National Park in the autumn, you can see and hear the elks bugle. It was there that my friend, Cliff Mills, told me the story of Samson, the trophy elk.

Samson was a twelve-year-old elk with a massive sixteen-point rack of antlers (seven points on one side and nine points on the other). He was likely the largest bull elk in Estes Valley. He was also the mascot at the YMCA camp just outside of town where he wintered every year.

The great elk showed no fear of humans and was quite approachable. He thought nothing of walking through people's yards and raiding the bird feeders on their front porches. In short, he was a local celebrity—the town's pet. However, all of that changed in the twilight hours of November 11, 1995.

A crossbow-toting poacher felled Samson with a single arrow near the entrance to the YMCA camp, which had about 1,100 guests and staff on the grounds at the time. They found Samson's body the next day. The poacher was caught, and he paid.

The convicted poacher received a 90-day jail term, 360 hours of public service (intensively supervised), $8,220 in fines and other charges, lost his Colorado driver's license for two years, is prohibited from hunting for at least six years, and is forbidden to own any weapon, "even a pocket knife."[6]

Dad was about to spin one of his favorite hunting stories.

Seems Dad had decided to camp in a big open meadow to get a head start on the next day's hunt. He was sound asleep and deep inside his sleeping bag when he had this sense that he wasn't alone. With sleep still heavy in his eyes, he looked in the general direction of his feet and the flap to his tent. There in the faint light of morning, he saw something. He slowly lifted his head. It was a buck, at least an eight-pointer, with his nose inside the tent! For a long, breathless moment, both of them held perfectly still. Dad gathered his thoughts as he formulated a plan of action. The deer had a plan of his own.

Dad grabbed his rifle as he fought his way out of his sleeping bag. The buck was halfway across the meadow by the time Dad got clear of the tent. Still, he took off across the meadow, hoping for a clean shot.

Ever try to run down a deer? It can't be done. Dad began to realize that fact after racing barefoot about a hundred yards through the open meadow in his long johns. It took him no time at all to cover that distance when all he could think about was that buck. The trip back was another matter.

Between Dad and his boots was a hundred yards of stickers, thistles, nettles, and sharp rocks. He spent the better part of the morning trying to pick his way around all the pointy things he'd somehow missed on his initial rush across the meadow. I'm pretty sure that was the only deer he saw on that trip. Just as well. It was several days before he could walk normally again.

If you get focused and moving fast enough, so the theory goes, you won't feel the rough spots. I have a similar theory regarding speed bumps, but it needs more work . . . along with the suspension on my car.

When you go hunting, you may not find what you were looking for, but you always find something. A friend of mine thinks God blinds us to the cost of some things so we'll enter the fray full-hearted—even if we have to stick our fingers in our ears, build a fire, and tiptoe through the stickers when it doesn't pan out the way we'd hoped.

WHAT MY DAD TAUGHT ME

The point of adventures is not knowing how they will turn out.

> *The really happy man is the one who can enjoy*
> *the scenery when he has to take a detour.*

HoW To RuiN A
PAiR oF TeNNiS SHoES

For as long as I can remember, I've enjoyed the feel of warm air blowing on my face. Give me a cold and blustery winter night and a good heat source any day. I love to hog the heat.

When I was small, I used to curl up in the front floorboard of our green Nash Rambler right under the heater vent. I could travel that way for hours, with the heated air blasting in my face on a long winter's drive.

When Mom was a first-grade teacher at Whittier Elementary on Pine Street, I often hung around her classroom after school. If it were winter, I'd lay on top of the radiators near the windows, scrunching my body up so that it covered the vents. I'd tuck my arms under my chest, close my eyes, and let the warm air play off my eyelids and lightly burn my face and the creases in the palms of my open hands. Sometimes I'd drift back into the memory of one particular Christmas when the Stanley clan had gathered in Shamrock, Texas, to celebrate the holiday. I was all of four or five years old at the time.

Mammuddy and Pop Pop heated their home with a giant floor furnace that creaked and groaned like some foul beast locked away in the earthen cellar. It had one large grate that sat just off center between the living and dining rooms. Somehow that one grate was supposed to heat the entire house. It didn't. Move into the other rooms, and the ambient air cooled as drafts from weathered windows reminded you that winter was just outside. That grate was my favorite spot in the house. When the furnace kicked on, the hot air called my name.

Grates aren't comfortable things to sit, squat, or stand on. The thin metal edges of the square openings slowly cut into your feet—like walking barefoot on gravel too early in the summer before your feet have had a chance to toughen up. Even with socks on, the discomfort of the grate would force me to abandon my perch long before I was ready to go. So on this particular cold winter night, I stood in the middle of the grate wearing a pair of Keds sneakers.

As I stood with my legs apart, the hot air which originated deep in the bowels of the house drifted up the legs of my blue jeans. Face down, eyes closed, I breathed in the heated air and smelled just a hint of heating oil. My face was flush. Red and yellow lights danced behind closed eyelids as I pushed the limits of what I could stand. Warmed to the bone on the high plains in the dead of winter, the sounds of the family receded into the background. If you've read the "Cremation of Sam McGee," you know just how I felt. Life was good.

Just as I reached the moment when I knew I'd have to retreat from the floor furnace, a new smell assaulted my senses. At first it was only a subtle wisp, almost indistinguishable from the lingering hint of fuel oil. But the odor quickly moved from mildly suspicious to full-bodied obnoxious—burning rubber! Pungent, nause-ating, sizzling, disgusting! I opened my eyes and looked around for the source of the odor. It was me! Or more accurately, my tennis shoes.

The soft rubber soles of my Keds had slowly melted into the square openings of the grate during my sauna. The smell and sizzle came from the stringy drops of tennis shoe tread slowly descending into the flames of the furnace. I nearly fell over; I

WHAT'S IN A NAME?

Keds was the first mass-marketed, rubber-soled, canvas-topped shoe. The manufacturers wanted to call their new product "Peds" (after the Latin word for foot). However, another company already held a trademark for that name. They decided to make up a new word reminiscent of the Latin term, and "Keds" was born. In the same spirit of inventiveness, an advertising agent named Henry Nelson McKinney coined the term "sneakers" in 1917 as a way of promoting the stealthy quietness of the new rubber-soled shoe.[7]

couldn't pull free. Stuck and sweating, I stood, the edge of the grate and safety looked hopelessly far off. Skewered over an open flame! Slow roasted like a holiday turkey! My last Christmas ever!

I may have been the first to smell the stink, but it didn't remain a secret for long. Soon my aunts, uncles, and cousins—the whole family—were investigating the sizzle and smell. It didn't take them long to discover who was the source of the problem.

Grandmother quickly turned off the furnace. Dad looked at my startled face and started to laugh. They all laughed. He straddled that big grate and lifted me straight up in the air. Plucpk! Pulled me right out of my shoes, spun me around, and carried me to the cooler regions of the surrounding hardwood floor. Dad checked my stockinged feet. No burns. Not so much as a blister.

After the grate cooled down, Dad and I sat at the edge and scraped burnt shoe rubber out of the tiny openings. We couldn't get it all and eventually decided the best option was to let the furnace finish what it had begun. I imagine Mammuddy lit a scented candle or two to mask the stench.

Looking back, I realize that no one made me pay for my mistake. No one seemed embarrassed or felt the need to embarrass or shame me. Dad didn't scold me for something I couldn't have foreseen. It was just one of those events that added to the family journal of unwritten wisdom: "Overindulgence stinks," "It takes longer to clean up than it does to mess up," and "You can't foresee every eventuality."

WHAT MY DAD TAUGHT ME

You are more important than any inconvenience or stink you happen to start.

> *If you survive childhood you'll have*
> *enough to write about for a lifetime.*
>
> —*Flannery O'Conner*

CATCH AND RELEASE—THE ONES THAT GOT AWAY

How to Train a Fish

For some folks, fishing is poetry in motion—a fly rod whipping the air with your own hand-tied fly on the end of an all but invisible leader. It is an art form in which a five-pound trout is landed on a three-pound test line after an hour-long contest, a mystical experience where the location of great fishing holes is a well-guarded secret shared only with the elect. You can learn a lot about life from fishing, especially if there's someone around to make sure you do.

I don't think Dad ever owned a fly rod. What he had was a no-nonsense fishing pole and a tackle box full of hooks, sinkers, floats, and a few lures he seldom found a use for. I still have them, although I haven't used them in years.

It didn't matter to Dad if the fishing was in a river or a lake or whether the fish were partial to worms, Red-Hots, or lures that day. As long as you got your line wet, you were fishing, and if you just happened to scoop something out of the river without the aid of a hook, well, that counted too. No one would ever confuse either one of us for great fishermen, but we had our moments—especially when it came to catch and release.

Dad once stocked the pond behind our house. "When they get big enough to eat, we can have fish any night we want," he boasted. And for the next month, he proceeded to catch and release just about every baby fish he put in that pond.

By the time those fish were big enough to eat, they'd all been caught and released so many times they were uncatchable. "Who would have thought you could train a fish!" he laughed. "Fishing is one of those things that can go along as predictable as you please, and then something unforeseeable happens. Guess that's why folks fish."

Weighed Down Waders

A few years later, we were fishing a stream near Boulder, Colorado, and Dad brought along his waders. The thought that you could walk through water and not get wet was pretty appealing. I watched him negotiate the middle of the stream, casting far beyond what I could reach from the bank. I eventually convinced him to let me have a go.

You could have put two of me in those heavy rubber waders. By the time I was strapped in, the waders' waist came up to my armpits. I was only nine or ten years old and looked like a pair of legs with a head attached.

It's not easy to walk through running water. Forget about fishing! There were slick rocks, unseen holes, a fishing pole to negotiate, and the current to contend with. On top of that, the air inside the waders gave them an unstable buoyancy that messed up my coordination. Just about the time I thought I had the hang of it, I slipped, and the one thing you don't ever want to happen, happened. The top of my waders dipped below the surface of the water.

In an instant, the waders had scooped up enough water to fill a good-size wading pool. I was encased in gallons and gallons of ice-cold water and flopping downstream. I couldn't get up in the waders. Couldn't get out of the waders. Couldn't get back to shore. I just floundered around on my hands and knees sputtering water. Forget wading! Forget hanging onto the fishing pole. The trick now was to gulp more air than water! It happened so fast that I didn't even have time to yell.

Dad must have seen me go down. I guess he thought he'd keep an eye on me rather than fish downstream. He jumped in and had hold of me in a second, but I was still in trouble. There was no way he could pick me up, so he dragged me, the waders, and about thirty gallons of water back to the side of the river. Once I was beached and breathing, he peeled me out of the waders that were stuck like glue to my wet clothes. Who'd have thought you could drown in a pair of waders in a stream that was two or three feet deep?

We sat in the sun and dried out right down to the elastic bands in our underwear (which never dries out as long as you're wearing them) and thought about what we were going to tell Mom. We were through fishing for the day, and I didn't mind one bit being the only thing Dad caught that afternoon. Come to think of it, I was the biggest catch he ever landed. Sure glad he didn't let me get away—catch and release at its best.

Hogtied by an Inner Tube

Years later I was surrounded by rubber in the middle of another rushing river—only this time it was on purpose. I was tubing Boulder Canyon with my buddy, Mike. We loved to tube and were always on the outlook for a good used inner tube suitable for bouncing off rocks and sailing down small falls. Mike had found a doozy—a big truck-tire inner tube you could really hunker down in and still keep your tailbone out of range of the boulders submerged just under the surface.

We'd just finished one of the more challenging parts of the canyon and were relaxing in a wide, slow bend in the river. Mike was cocooned inside his big inner tube, and I was draped more or less on top of my regular tube as we drifted side by side, eyes half closed. The roar of the canyon faded as we floated along. But over the sound of the water I heard, "Ooosh." It wasn't much of a noise, but it just didn't fit with the other sounds of the river.

I looked around for the source and saw nothing unusual. Still, something wasn't right. And then it dawned on me what I wasn't seeing—Mike. Just a second before, he was floating right next to me and now he was gone!

I did a three-hundred-and-sixty-degree turn in my inner tube to see if he'd floated behind me. Still no Mike. Outside of an alien abduction, there was no way he could have vanished so quickly without a trace. And then I saw it—his nose!

GREAT WATER ESCAPES AND THE PATENT OFFICE

Dad, an amateur magician who could talk a great trick even if he couldn't do one, loved to regale me with stories of Harry Houdini.

Houdini made his name as an escape artist, often performing his escapes while hanging upside down from a great height or in water.

Houdini's interest in underwater breathing apparatuses led to an interesting fact that often escapes notice. Houdini holds U.S. Patent Number 1,370,316. It reads:

> "The invention relates to deep sea diving suits or armors, and its object is to provide a new and improved diver's suit arranged to permit the diver, in case of danger for any cause whatever, to quickly divest himself of the suit while being submerged and to safely escape and reach the surface of the water."

Houdini's invention and interest in self-contained underwater breathing apparatuses (today known as SCUBA diving) likely contributed to more than a few water escapes long after he was gone. He was the greatest catch-release artist of them all![8]

Mike's nose was bobbing along the surface of the water a few feet to my right. I jumped out of my tube and found the rest of Mike under his nose. I couldn't begin to pick him up, but I got his head above water and dragged him over to the side of the river—much as my dad had done for me all those years ago.

He looked so ridiculous that his near drowning soon gave way to guffaws. He'd been hogtied by his own inner tube!

Mike had run into a sharp piece of metal, probably the only one in Boulder Creek, and suffered a blowout. He was sitting so low in the tube that when it suddenly contracted, the inner tube cinched his knees to his chest, trapped his arms next to his body, and pushed his head down into his knees. Mike had been able to push just hard enough to get his chin up and his nose above the waterline for me to see.

Once I got him beached, it was clear he wasn't going to drown, but he also wasn't going anywhere. Extricating him from the mouth of the inner tube was like wrestling an inert python that had already swallowed its prey. We had to work from both sides of the problem to get him out. I was briefly tempted to leave him just where he was until I could find a camera.

Pulling Mike to shore wasn't the only time I happened to be there when someone else was in desperate need of help, and the day I nearly drowned in Dad's waders wasn't the only time I've nearly died. There's a lot more catch and release going on around us than we are aware of. But when we do take note, we find the gift of life has more meaning than it did before.

Winston Churchill once said, "There is nothing more invigorating than to be shot at to no effect." I've learned a similar truth on more than one occasion in the middle of a river.

WHAT MY DAD TAUGHT ME

Life is a gift that is given to us over and over again by the benevolent Fisher of men.

> *Our God is a God who saves; from the*
> *Sovereign LORD comes escape from death.*
>
> —*Psalm 68:20 NIV*

A GRAVEYARD TALE FOR THE GULLIBLE

A good storyteller isn't a slave to facts, but he also doesn't hide the possibility that some of his own inventions may have been added for flavor either. Dad was a natural-born storyteller, but you had to be careful of how much of his tales you swallowed.

I couldn't begin to count the number of times I asked a question only to have him inquire, "Are you sure you have no idea what the answer might be?" A positive response from me would all but guarantee that an answer would be invented on the spot for me and anyone else gullible enough to swallow it. Often as not, he'd dip into his collection of urban myths—like the time I wanted to know how people found superhuman strength in times of great need.

• • •

Seems there was this fella who routinely took a shortcut through an old graveyard full of headstones and shade trees. It had a wrought-iron gate at both ends and dozens of meandering paths in between. There was a certain randomness to it—no neat rows of markers that could be easily mowed around.

On this particular day he had to work late, but the unsettling nature of walking through a cemetery after dark was offset by his familiarity with the terrain. The moon and clouds vied for center stage as shadows faded into nothingness only to reappear moments later. He strolled along, paying little attention to his step. It had been a long day. What he couldn't know was that a new grave had been dug right in the middle of his shortcut.

Sure enough, he stumbled into the freshly dug hole. Once he realized what had happened and found himself uninjured, he set about to get out. He couldn't. The hole was too deep. He tried to brace his back against one side and his feet against the other and walk his way up. The width of the hole and looseness of the dirt negated all his efforts. He yelled for help. No one heard. Finally, he resigned himself to wait out the night and made himself as comfortable as possible in one corner of the hole.

Almost asleep, he heard someone whistling a cheerful tune. Apparently, he wasn't the only one who liked to cut through the cemetery. He started to yell and then thought better of it. *What if I scare him off? What if he walks by and*

URBAN MYTHS ON AN EMPTY TOMB

No graveyard escape has received more scrutiny than the Resurrection of Jesus Christ. Throughout the centuries, skeptics have tried to come up with some plausible explanation that avoids the miraculous conclusion that He physically rose from the dead.

The Swo-o-o-n Theory: Jesus only appeared to be dead and fooled His followers into thinking he'd risen from the dead. (Venturini came up with this story a couple of centuries ago.)

The Theft Theory: The disciples somehow stole the body from the tomb and convinced everyone that Jesus had risen from the dead. (See Matthew 28:11-15.)

The Hallucination Theory: People only imagined they shared meals, embraced, and spoke with Jesus after His death.

The Wrong Tomb Theory: Everyone went to the wrong tomb and no one ever noticed the mistake. (Kirsopp Lake has offered up this version.)

The Little or None of It Ever Happened Theory: The resurrection accounts were written, or rewritten, centuries later and are nothing more than a nice fiction. (The Jesus Seminar, founded in 1985.)

The Mistaken Identity Theory: Someone else died in Jesus' place or, as some Islamic literature suggests, Judas magically switched places with Jesus on the cross.[9]

I miss my chance to get out of here? He was still making up his mind when the whistler fell into the other end of the same hole.

The new occupant tried to get out of the hole with no more success than the first man. Feeling a bit sheepish about not announcing his presence to the new arrival sooner, he finally said, "I couldn't get out either. Perhaps we can help each other . . . "

He didn't get a chance to finish his sentence. His opening comment had barely passed his lips when the other man leaped out of the hole and fled into the night!

• • •

I never did get a precise answer to my question about the

source of superhuman strength. I suppose you could conclude that the second fella had more athletic ability than the first or that a kindly spirit haunting the graveyard gave him a hand. You might even conclude that adrenaline had something to do with it. I think Dad would tell you that the story has something to do with leaping to conclusions. And if you were to press him for a further explanation, you'd be more gullible than most.

WHAT MY DAD TAUGHT ME

Admitting one's ignorance can be good for the soul, but it opens the door to more than urban myths.

> *Never forget that you are a part of the*
> *people who can be fooled some of the time.*

MAKING ALLOWANCES

"If we're not having fun, we're probably doing something wrong." That was Dad's philosophy on most things. Life was an adventure to be embraced, not a sentence to be endured. And the mundane things of life were best learned in the form of a game.

We were on a day trip, exploring a frontier village replete with wooden sidewalks, gunfights, and curio shops. I was wearing my chaps, boots, and cowboy hat for the occasion and hauling my entire savings along with me (just in case I ran across something I couldn't live without). Literally every cent I had was in my pockets. I could hardly keep my pants up. I was strictly a hard-currency man. I jingled as I swaggered down the boardwalk without the aid of spurs.

After watching me hitch up my pants every few steps, Dad said, "Gary, how about swapping your coins with me?" He pocketed my mess of coins and gave me a couple of dollar bills in exchange.

What just happened? The reassuring weight of prosperity had just vanished. My load had been lightened along with my net worth. *I've just been swindled! Held up! BY MY DAD!*

We hadn't gone far when Mom noticed all was not well with her only son. "What's wrong, Gary?"

"Daddy took all my money!" I blubbered.

Daddy tried to reassure me that I had come out ahead in the deal, but I wasn't buying the notion that a couple pieces of paper could possibly be worth as much as my horde of coins.

Dad returned my coins, and I spent the rest of the day hitchin' up my pants as we explored the Old West.

A few days later, Dad announced, "Gary, it's up to you to pick how much allowance you get. You can have all the coins concealed in either my right or left hand. I'll show you both hands for a couple of seconds, and then you have to choose."

Back in those days, a decent allowance ranged between a dime and a quarter. The prospect of improving my weekly take was appealing, and I eyeballed his hands with all the intensity of a bomb-squad officer about to defuse an explosive.

He opened both hands, and I quickly surveyed a mix of pennies, nickels, and dimes. All too soon, he closed his hands and said, "Okay, Gary, which hand do you choose?" Being about five at the time, I went for volume on that first outing. Dad laid both handfuls of coins on the table in two piles, and we added them up.

I learned that day that quantity isn't always the best way to judge value. The pile of pennies I chose (with a couple of nickels mixed in) was several cents less than the two dimes in the other pile.

We played that game once a week for several months until I could add up any combination of coins in a heartbeat. (I only picked the lesser allowance once after that first try.)

When math classes rolled around in grade school, Dad taught me how to play a solitaire card game in which you collect pairs of cards adding up to thirteen. Under Dad's gaming approach to mathematics, I easily negotiated my way

ALLOWANCES AREN'T WHAT THEY USED TO BE

According to an Ohio State University study done in 1999 and a 1998 *Consumer Reports* survey:

- Eight-year-olds have allowances that average less than $4 per week (throw in gifts and other income, and the amount grows to $16.40 a week).

- Twelve-year-olds average $6.66 per week in allowances (include gifts and other income, and the amount increases to $30.95 a week).

- The typical teen allowance averages $50 a week.

- Every week Americans are giving their children more than $1 billion in allowances.

No wonder so much advertising is targeted at these age groups![10]

through the world of numbers. I may never have won a spelling contest, but I seldom lost a math contest—way too much fun.

One of the oldest bits of advice regarding the assessment of value is to "number your days." Of course it all depends on your numbering system; pick the right one, and you'll successfully negotiate your way through life. Pick the wrong system, and you'll end up with a pocketful of change when you could have had the priceless gift of a wonderful life.

WHAT MY DAD TAUGHT ME

A good education not only can keep you from being swindled, it can't be taken away.

> *Most of the world's value systems are a frenzied attempt to collect art in a museum only to discover at the door that it all has to be returned.*

YOU DON'T HAVE TO COMPETE FOR LOVE

SECTION II

THE STAGES OF LIFE

Life comes in stages, or so the theory goes. In the early "external stages," you compete with yourself, and then others, and then with yourself again. The external stages are driven by the conviction that there is just so much power, wealth, and recognition to be had, and you'd better look out for number one, form advantageous alliances, and get while the getting is good.

The later "internal stages" see life differently. You quit competing with yourself as you discover that true success doesn't hinge on your limited abilities. You quit competing with others when you realize that there is a limitless supply of all the things that really matter—things like love and acceptance.[11]

BETWEEN HIS SHOULDERS

Quick now! Your house is on fire. You have no more than three minutes to get out. What do you take with you after the family and pets? Don't stop to think about it. No time. Move!

Time's up. What did you end up with out on the front sidewalk as you watch everything else go up in smoke? The television? Your portfolio? A keepsake or two? Nah, you've got the family photo album in your hands, don't you? Just about everything else is replaceable, but not those albums. They're really books of memories—often good memories. You probably wouldn't recall half of them without those visual reminders. There is just something about that little piece of celluloid that triggers synapses, fires neurons, and dredges up a smile to go with the photograph.

Aren't you glad now that Mom and Dad, or Aunt Judy, insisted on taking all those photos? At the time, it all seemed so torturous. You stand around and wait—feeling foolish, sun in your eyes, strangers staring. And there is Uncle so-and-so squinting through the viewfinder for a couple of millennium. Weeks later you get copies in the mail, and they sit in a drawer for ten years. Later someone in the family goes to an arts and crafts workshop on photo albums, scissors are bought that cut curlicues, and all of a sudden the photos are dug out and arranged in an album, looked at, and put back on the shelf for another decade.

Take them down. Thumb through them. Bet your heart will stir at something you see—something you remember that has long lain forgotten. You might need to write a letter or pick up the phone or say a prayer.

That happened to me the other day. I found a photograph of me when I was two years old. It surprised me. Turns out that Mom and Dad took me to Colorado when I was a tot. I have no memory of the event. But there I am sitting on Dad's shoulders on the top of Pikes Peak. We're talkin' up there!

Pikes Peak is 14,110 feet above sea level. On a clear day, you can practically see Kansas. Add to that Dad's 6' 2". I figure if I'm riding on his shoulders I must be what? Ten miles high!

While that particular photograph evoked no specific memory of *that* day, I have many memories of riding on my daddy's shoulders. Raised overhead like the Stanley Cup after winning the big game, I was often lofted up into the stratosphere and prominently placed on the mantle of Dad's shoulders. Dad could walk for hours with me on his shoulders, his long, easy stride gobbling up the miles as I learned not to hang on too tight or use his neck for a saddle horn.

I've read somewhere that it is good for the development of a child's inner ear to be tossed up in the air when they're little, held overhead, and perched on Daddy's shoulders. There is just something about seeing a baby twirling around in the air that makes everyone smile. (I also seem to remember an old German insult that says, "As a child he must have been thrown up in the air three times and caught twice." Be careful!)

One of the best things about riding on Dad's shoulders was the proximity of his curly, black hair. I'd

PiKES PEAK

Pikes Peak bears the name of a man who never managed to get to the top—Zebulon M. Pike (1806).

Katharine Lee Bates did make the ascent, however, and the summit inspired her to pen "America the Beautiful."

"Pikes Peak or Bust" became synonymous with the Colorado Gold Rush, but it doesn't seem as if anyone ever found any gold worth mentioning on the mountain itself.

In 1901 the first automobile (the Locomobile Steamer by Yony and Felker) made it to the top after nine hours of pushing and driving.

The current record for the Pikes Peak Hill Climb (formerly the Race to the Clouds) was set by Rod Millen in 1994. I wonder how often, during those 10 minutes and 4.06 seconds of hairpin turns and hundred-foot drop-offs, Ron felt he was about to be tossed in the air and wondered if he'd be caught.[12]

run my fingers through it, rearrange it, fluff it, make it look silly. Then I'd move to other objects of interest—like his ears. Like a pair of reins, I'd pull on one of his ears, and we'd turn that direction, or I'd pull on the other and we'd go the other way. It's different from being carried on your mom's hip or cradled in your parent's arms. Up top, you have a sense of where you are going. When we were negotiating our way through a crowd of people, I could see what Dad couldn't, and I became our guide. We were a team in which he did all the work. His strength and stature were transferred to me.

There is something about being way up high that still intrigues me—draws me to the edge of life for a better look. Perched up on Daddy's shoulders in a crowd, I could watch the parade, see the game, and not worry about getting stepped on. So exposed yet so safe. Wise men have called this "dwelling between your father's shoulders." That's the way it's supposed to be. Picked up, carried, tossed in the air and always caught—that is where the inner ear of trust is developed.

WHAT MY DAD TAUGHT ME

We borrow strength from those we're closest to. The closer you get, the safer you are; the safer you are, the more you can dare.

> *Photos used to be a way of freezing reality.*
> *Now they're a way of thawing imagination.*
>
> —Jaron Lanier

BiOLOGiCAL iMPOSSiBiLiTiES

i am a biological impossibility—something about one good tube and one good ovary but both connected to their inadequate counterparts. Never made much sense to me. Still, being a biological impossibility has its advantages.

My folks were convinced that I was a "miracle baby," and the first thing programmed into my wee brain was, "You are a miracle, a gift from God." I expect that's true of everyone, but it was nice to hear it from the two people who defined my world.

Mom quit her teaching job the month she found out she was pregnant. She wanted to savor the whole experience. Inside of her was the answer to a long held prayer. She and Dad had been married for thirteen years before I came along.

Of course, everyone in the family was eager to welcome me into the world, including my grandmother, Alma McGowen. Alma was a strong woman of faith and gumption, a poet and songwriter. She had also been a one-room schoolteacher, a rancher's wife, and a widow. When her husband died in the Great Influenza Plague of 1918, she was left alone to raise three children, all under the age of four.

At the end of her life, when she was dying of cancer, she didn't want her youngest daughter, my mother, to know. Keeping the hard things from each other was a family trait. Propped up in a bed miles away from where Mom was in labor and fanned by her other daughter, Judy, she helped to pray me into this world. The day I was born, she turned to Judy and said, "Myrtle has a baby boy. They're both fine." Fifteen minutes later, Dad called to confirm what she already knew.

Why God gave her firsthand knowledge of the events of my birth rather than leaving it to a phone call from Dad, I don't know. I was seven days old when Alma McGowen departed this life for a better one. I only know her through the stories that have been handed down, like her inside information about me—the "miracle baby."

We each have a story surrounding our birth, but mine packed some confusion into my life regarding the nature of biology and divine intervention. One day, as our old Nash Rambler hit the downhill side of Broadway that runs past the fraternity houses in Boulder, I asked Dad, "I'm an answer to prayer, aren't I? A miracle baby?"

"You sure are, Gary," he answered his seven-year-old son.

"Well, I understand that Mom is my mother; I came out of her stomach. But how is it that you are my dad rather than God being my dad?" I was thinking that if God is the One who answers prayers and that's what I am, then He must be my father. Besides, I was well versed in the Christmas story and *that* miraculous birth. I caught Dad off guard.

Dad tried to fashion an answer that confirmed both truths. He assured me that he was indeed my dad, and that God was very much the Father of us all. "Sometimes God lets us participate in the miracles He performs," he said. "He let me be a part of the miracle that created

THE OTHER DADDY

It was the toughest moment in His life. He knew what was coming—the betrayal, the beatings, His own barbaric death. There was no way around it. The grief was so great He wept not tears, but blood. And in that moment in the garden, the most intimate word ever uttered escaped His lips—"Daddy."

No one had ever dared to use such a familiar and common term with the Creator of the Universe, the Eternal Father, the Righteous Judge, God Almighty. The man who wept in a garden that night had called God "Father" hundreds of times in the hearing of His listeners. Some were offended. "What makes God your Father?" they sneered. Well, He was the only begotten Son. God was His father in a way no one else could ever claim.

"You'd like My Daddy," Jesus invites. "I'd really like to share Him with you. Unbelievable as it sounds, He loves you every bit as much as He loves Me. And more than anything, He longs for you to know Him as Daddy."[13]

you, and I am your father in a way that no one else ever could be."

We were two or three years away from the facts-of-life talk which would mix zygotes, eggs, and sperm with love, commitment, and prayer. He knew I didn't need a complete answer to my innocent question that day. But in a way, his first answer has been more useful than the biological one that came later.

WHAT MY DAD TAUGHT ME

I have two daddies—we all do.

The deepest search in life . . . was man's search to find a father, not merely the father of his flesh, . . . but the image of a strength and wisdom external to his need and superior to his hunger, to which the belief and power of his own life could be united.

—Thomas Wolfe

i KNEW YOU'D REMEMBER!

*B*efore the advent of television, all-day Sunday soccer tournaments, and the repeal of Sunday blue laws, going to church was a regular part of life. My folks went just about every time the doors were open. They taught Sunday school and Training Union classes, led youth group, and even found time for Wednesday night visitation. You name it, and they probably did it at one time or another, except for singing in the choir. Church life had a certain rhythm and routine that seldom changed.

Ever notice how your car knows the way home, even when you weren't planning on going home? Before you know it, you're driving up your street and thinking, *Wait a minute! I'm supposed to be picking up the clothes from the dry cleaners!* It isn't easy to override the mental automatic pilot located between the ears.

It was Wednesday night, and Mom and Dad were out visiting the visitors from last Sunday's services. They made the rounds, invited folks back to church, and generally tried to make the new-comers feel at home. They'd done it count-less times before. First, those who were going out on visitation would gather at church, have a cup of coffee, divvy up the names according to location, pray, and then go.

Having a baby was a new thing for my folks. Married for thirteen years before I came along, they'd settled into a number of non-baby routines. After they finished visiting those on their list, they went home and settled in for the night. Two hours later, a tiny voice in the

MEMORY MYTHS

In his book, *Memory: Remembering and Forgetting in Everyday Life*, Dr. Barry Gordon debunks the first five myths about memory loss. They include:

Myth 1: Forgetfulness is evidence that there's a problem with your brain.
Reality: The ability to selectively store and discard memories is essential. If we remembered every single event, it would destroy our mental health.

Myth 2: Every day your brain loses ten-thousand brain cells and eventually there will be nothing left to remember with.
Reality: We do lose brain cells every day but not in the area where our thought processes occur. (We also develop new brain cells throughout life.)

Myth 3: The more stressed you are about losing your memory, the more serious it is likely to be.
Reality: The more bothered you are about memory problems, the less likely it is that you actually have problems with memory (though anxiety itself can contribute to the inability to retrieve memories easily).

Myth 4: The best way to tell if your memory is normal is to compare it to other folks' memory abilities.
Reality: There is such a wide range of ability in this area that "normal" for you may well be quite different from someone else's "normal."

Myth 5: If you are worried that you may have Alzheimer's, you probably do.
Reality: The family and friends of Alzheimer's patients worry about memory loss; the patients themselves usually don't.[14]

back of their minds began to whisper, "Haven't you forgotten something? Isn't there some unfinished business yet to attend to?" Then it hit them.

"We left Gary at the church nursery, which closed hours ago!"

They rushed back to find the light on, back door unlocked, and the sitter rocking me. "I knew you'd eventually remember you had a baby," she said.

That was the only time it ever happened. I was never forgotten again. The nursery worker never forgot either and delighted in reminding my parents, years down the road, of the night they went home without me.

I wish I could say the night I was left at the nursery marked me as one who always remembers. It didn't. I've stood up a lot of folks, left a few behind, and not kept my word. I was too busy, living on automatic—too caught up in my own life. Still, there's something in all of us that longs to be remembered.

"Remember me," was the plea of at least one criminal about to depart this life as he hung on a cross next to the most famous cross of all. He was remembered. It made all the difference. It still does.

WHAT MY DAD TAUGHT ME

Don't kick yourself when you forget—the limp just slows you down.

> *It isn't necessary to remember your mistakes;*
> *there will always be those who are happy*
> *to remember them for you.*
>
> —Gary Stanley

SWIMMING ON DADDY'S BACK

"You have to believe that the water will spend more time holding you up than it spends pulling you under," Dad instructed.

It is hard to "believe" when your experience is telling you something else.

"Relax. Don't fight the water; move through it. Keep your mouth shut, your eyes open, and your fingers together."

Dad's words were all but useless. Surrounded by water, an odd mix of excitement and fear gripped me. Everything in me wanted to thrash and flail.

"I've got you, Gary. I won't let anything happen," Dad continued as he supported my small body with his hand.

While I couldn't relax in the water, I could always relax in his hand—and I soon did. The unknown became comfortable in the company of the known, and progress was made in the absence of panic. Dad's presence was stronger than my surroundings. And it wasn't long before I was ready to believe that the water actually would spend more time holding me up than it spent pulling me under. I loved the water, and I loved to swim, especially when Dad was around.

"Grab your nose, grab your knees, and take a deep breath!" And with that bit of instruction Dad began to spin me somersault style in about five feet of water. My head shot down and then back up as I made my first complete forward somersault; air and water in the face, a giant hand behind the neck, and the other hand pushing the front of my ankles like the helm of an old pirate ship. The first time we tried it, I only made one revolution before I came out of my tuck and ended the spin cycle, unsure of which way was up. But over time my lung capacity improved right along with Dad's technique. My lifetime record was twenty-two complete revolutions on one breath.

Dad was a great floater. At 210 pounds he displaced a lot of water. He could propel himself along feet first with his toes out of the water, and when he did, look out! Crab Toe might get you! Dad had perfected the pinching skill necessary to grab the skin around my middle between his big toe and the next one. When crab toe was out and about, the goal was to swim as close as you could without getting caught. We played "crab tag" a thousand times.

"Rest your hands on my shoulders, and don't choke me. Remember, let the water hold you up." Hitching a ride on Daddy's back was like bodysurfing through slow waves. Each of his frog kicks propelled us forward as we dropped lower in the water, and each breaststroke lifted us higher again. I soon learned that if I pushed myself too far out of the water, the added weight forced Dad to swim harder, and my ride was shortened. But if I lay as close as I could, the water supporting my weight, he could swim forever. I tried to make myself so light he'd hardly notice I was there—swimming on Daddy's back.

Luci and I had lunch the other day with some new friends, Doug and Amy. They recently adopted two brothers, five and seven years old. Amy told us of the first time she took them to the community pool. "I won't let anything happen to you," Amy assured her two new sons. Just remember that your arm floaties (the modern version of water wings) will keep you up."

The younger one took to the water with his arm floaties like a

THE REMARKABLE THING ABOUT WATER

Water is the most common substance on earth (it covers about 75 percent of the earth's surface), but it is also the number one exception to the rule. Water is the only known substance whose solid state—ice—is less dense than its liquid state. That's why lakes freeze from the top down rather than the bottom up—a very good thing for fish and the rest of us. If ice sank, the oceans would freeze from the bottom up, and the earth would be an arctic desert.

Water is the only substance normally found as a liquid, gas, and solid on the surface of the planet. Water can absorb more heat without noticeable change to its structure than anything except ammonia. Water can support things heavier than itself by surface tension and even pull against gravity. But best of all, you can swim in it.[15]

baby duck. He knew something about trust because he has always had his big brother to look out for him. But the older boy was terrified of the water. Years of foster care had taught him that adults weren't all that trustworthy.

It took several days just to coax him to the edge of the pool where he sat with his feet in the water. Eventually, he allowed Amy to hold him as he clung to her and she stood in the water next to the side of the pool. Then they worked up to the point where she could take him a single step away from the side and then right back again. The day he dog-paddled a whole five feet from Amy's arms back to Doug's embrace, he shouted, "I trusted you! I trusted you, Mommy!"

The boy didn't say, "These arm floaties really work!" though that was true. No, his newfound trust was wrapped tightly around a person—his new mom. Before any of us can act on the promise that "the arm floaties will hold you up," or that "the water will spend more time holding you up than pulling you under," we have to believe the one saying those words. Sometimes it only takes a moment; sometimes it takes a lot longer. Either way, trust is always personal.

WHAT MY DAD TAUGHT ME

Whether you're holding on for dear life or trying to keep a feather touch so light it's hardly noticed, it's the object of your faith, not the size of it, that matters.

Trust is like a finely lacquered finish,
it is built up one layer at a time.

A LOVE FOR
THE FLOOR

Remember the old television advertisement with two corporate types rushing through an airport? They pass a lost-looking little boy on their way to the plane. The older exec stops and stoops down to the boy's level to see if everything is all right. Everything is not all right—with the young executive. Seeing his boss lingering with the boy when he ought to be lunging for the gate, he blurts out, "My God! We've got a plane to catch!"

The boy looks up into the kind eyes of the distinguished, gray-haired man and asks, "Are you God?"

The little boy already has his suspicions. An adult on his own level, bending an adult schedule around a child's quandary? Never happened before! The boy is well rehearsed in the twin mantras that "Big boys don't cry," and "Children should be seen but not heard." Seems likely that it would take a divine being to so blatantly break man's conventions. Maybe this man with the kind eyes really is God. Easy to see how the child could mistake an expletive for exultation. If it were real life, I'd be willing to entertain the possibility that the guy was at least an angel—or a daddy.

The meaningful moments with children take place when you enter their world . . . on the floor . . . in the dirt. If you never bend the knee or wrinkle your perfectly pressed trousers, you'll never be in a position to embrace life. Life is messy, and the carefully kept aren't ready for it. It's inconvenient. You may well miss the plane, lose the deal, be thought unprofessional. But then, you might also be mistaken for God if you do.

A friend of mine learned this lesson from his daughter's crayon drawings. She always drew him as a head on top of two legs with no body. It finally hit him that from her perspective, that's exactly how he looked— a head peering down from atop two long legs at the little girl at his feet. He set about to change that picture of himself. He stooped. He got down on her level and showed his heart.

I know about floor-loving daddies. I had one. We wrestled, snuggled, and tickled on the floor. We were a daring acrobatic duo in a circus. Dad would lie on his back with his knees in the air, and I would balance there on my stomach as he spun me around with his hands and knees. I even performed death-defying headstands on his stomach as he held the rest of me straight in the air. But best of all, we Indian wrestled.

Indian wrestling is like thumb wrestling except that you use your whole body. You lay on your backs, side by side, hip to hip, facing in opposite directions. Then you grab forearms and raise your inside leg in the air three times. The third time, you lock ankles and try to flip the other person by pulling their leg back over their head.

Mom was the reigning champ in our home. Quick and savvy, she'd make her opponents (Dad and me) reach too far back to lock ankles, and the next thing you'd know, you were doing backward somersaults. Indian wrestling has little to do with size and everything to do with timing and strategy (something my football-playing roommate discovered in our dorm room one night to his great surprise).

Carpet burns and noogies are visible reminders that love is a touchable thing.

THE SERIOUS BUSINESS OF PLAY

Study any book on temperament types, and you'll soon discover that people with different temperaments approach play differently. At one end of the spectrum, you have the temperament types who never feel like they have to earn the right to play. At the other end of the spectrum, you have the types who seriously schedule in a certain amount of play into their lives because it is supposed to be a healthy exercise—in moderation.

Play is serious business either way you slice it because it awakens in children their imagination and wonder of discovery. The same holds true for adults. Play releases life-giving energy and removes the dullness that settles over our lives when we are preoccupied with the pressures and responsibilities of an adult world.[16]

WHAT MY DAD TAUGHT ME

Love that doesn't enter the other person's world is little more than a nice thought between your ears.

> *There is no exercise better for the heart*
> *than reaching down and lifting people up.*
>
> —John Andrew Holmer

THE KEYS TO EVERYTHING

" have two magical devices," boasted Dad one afternoon. "One allows you to actually see through walls, and the other will allow you to physically pass through a solid wall. Want to know what they are?"

"Sure!" Who wouldn't? Sounded like something from the Arabian Nights—our own Abracadabra-something-or-other. To be able to see what's on the other side is a temptation hard to resist.

Dad held out his right hand, turned it over palm up and back palm down. He rolled up his sleeve with all the flourish of a master magician and reached into his front pants pocket. He frowned, bit his lower lip, and made a show of searching for something mysterious. Slowly, he withdrew his hand and rubbed the back of it with the index finger of his other hand. "I now hold in my right hand a magical bit of metal that will allow me to walk right through the front wall of our house!" And with that, he opened his hand to show me his house key.

"Oh, Daddy! That's not magic. That's just an old key!"

"Really?" he asked. "To one who has never seen a key, it would be magical indeed. Perhaps you're just too familiar with it to savor how truly remarkable it is."

He was right about one thing; it would allow one to pass through a wall. But I was expecting something else—something wonderful and mysterious. Now on guard, I began to think about his "magical" device for seeing through walls—nothing came to mind.

"How can you see through walls?" I asked, with far less enthusiasm than I'd had moments before.

In response, he quickly moved to the window and drew back the curtains. "Voila!" he exclaimed. "I give you the window, a wondrous device that allows one to see right through walls!"

Dad had a way of looking around the edges of life that turned the ordinary into the extraordinary. His favorite question was, "What do you see?" He never tired of exploring the world through the eyes of his son. And on occasion, I also challenged the way he saw life, not with my answers but my actions. Like the time I set him on the road to a "key" discovery of his own during a morning romp across a field.

Construction sites are a blend of newly dug dirt, "green" concrete, the smell of cut wood, and tall weeds. Edgecliff subdivision was only a couple of gravel roads, a handful of scattered houses in various stages of construction, and Daddy's dreams.

Most mornings, the sound of the construction crew drifted across the fields and joined us for breakfast. I was five years old. Howdy Doody ruled Saturday morning television, and a cute little redheaded girl lived next door. It was also the beginning of my jaunts with Dad to inspect his construction sites and learn the trade.

I suspect a five-year-old can be a handful at a building site. There's just way too much to get into. There are nails to step on, walls to fall off of, holes to fall into, and dangerous stuff at every turn. Keeping me occupied and out of trouble was undoubtedly a major consideration in those early days, and distractions played a key role. Distractions tend to play themselves out in one of two ways: harmless but time-consuming or dangerous and costly. On this occasion, we stumbled into a combination of both.

Dad had collected all of the keys to the subdivision on a huge key ring. It must have weighed a couple of pounds—not the sort of thing you could keep in your pocket. I think Dad must have carried them on his belt.

One gray morning in early fall, he decided to let me carry them. All those keys clanging together! I was a one-man band—timpani, xylophone, and cymbals all wrapped up in one. Together we marched across the open field, picking our way around the taller weeds and muddy spots, headed for a small bonfire where the building crew gathered on their breaks.

We warmed ourselves by the fire, talked and laughed with the guys, and got something warm to drink. "Gary, where are the keys? We need to get into one of the houses before the inspector comes."

Keys? I had them a minute ago. How could I lose anything that big and noisy? "I don't know!" I cried.

Dad couldn't believe I'd lost them either. His face was a mixture of surprise and incredulity. "Look in your pockets. Did you set them down?" he asked.

No amount of verbal coaxing could empower me to produce what I'd lost. The order of business changed for the day. Everyone on the building site began to search for the keys to the subdivision. Our search quickly spread from the bonfire to the field we'd recently crossed. We retraced our steps, fanned out, cordoned off various sections. Nothing worked. After an hour of fruitless searching, Dad resigned himself to the fact that the keys weren't going to show up any time soon. I felt sick. It was my fault . . . my responsibility. What now?

Dad shook his head, tousled my hair, and smiled. I don't remember what he said, but in those few gestures, he confirmed that I was more important than what I'd lost or any

DON'T POCKET YOUR KEYS

The key has been a symbol of status and power for a long time. We have keys for everything—the key to the city, the key to your heart, or the key to your new car. In ancient Egypt, the number of keys owned by the head of the household determined his importance. The more keys you had, the more wealth and authority you possessed. And it was easy to keep count back then—the keys were so large that slaves (key bearers) carried them on their shoulders for all to see.[17]

inconvenience I had caused. Keys can be replaced and locks changed, but sons are to be treasured. He called a locksmith who had to rekey every lock in the subdivision.

We never did find that wad of keys. I suspect they now reside on some distant planet along with my left contact lens, an assortment of odd socks, numerous pencils and pens, and dozens of scraps of paper on which I've written important phone numbers for calls I've yet to return.

I'm married to a woman who loses things. Keys, watches, and Daytimers simply vanish when she goes to retrieve them. One day I was consoling her on the loss of something or other when it hit me: Lost things can be a precursor to a party. Think about it. Jesus told the parables of a lost sheep, a lost coin, and a lost son; all ended in celebrations once they were found. It has started to change the way Luci and I go about looking for things we've misplaced. Instead of focusing on the frustration of time wasted and steps retraced, we're starting to look ahead to the celebration once it is found. I bet Dad would have come to the same conclusion.

WHAT MY DAD TAUGHT ME

Never entrust the keys to everything to a five-year-old, unless you have a second set.

> *"Seek and ye shall find" doesn't apply to everything, but it does apply to enough.*
>
> —Gary Stanley

SCRAMBLED EGGS AND COLD FEET

Morning rituals can become more than mere rituals; they can become the glue that holds much of life in place.

Mom and I were night owls. Dad wasn't. Along about 9:30 P.M., Dad's steel gray eyes would begin to flutter. His chin would drop. The effervescent side of Dad went into hibernation. Nonessential systems shut down for the evening. I can't recall a single late night conversation with my dad. Mornings were another story.

By 5:30 A.M., all systems were go as far as Dad was concerned. By 6:30, he had shaved, showered, and savored a few pages from the Bible that lived in the smallest room in our house. The smell of bacon would begin to waft through the house. Scrambled eggs would hit the skillet, and one important morning ritual would begin.

"Gary! Breakfast! Time to get up!"

Huh? Whatsersnafersoft. Z-z-z-z-z-z.

"Gary?"

Some days I'd just get up. Some days I'd take a walk on the wild side and stay in bed.

From the remotest edge of consciousness, the sound of running water trickled down my ear canal, bounced off my eardrum, and made its way to some part of my brain that noted its presence. I automatically burrowed deeper under the covers, still one with the mattress.

The sound of footsteps soon replaced that of running water as the well-worn ritual unfolded without variation or shifting shadow. The covers at the foot of my bed began to slowly lift. An unwelcome draft greeted my feet. *"Danger, Will Robinson! Danger!"* With all the mastery born of self-preservation, I giggled and spun in my bedding, wrapping it around me as tight as a cocoon around a reluctant butterfly.

"Here comes Mr. Washcloth! Ooh, he's cold! Bet he'd like to find something warm to take off the morning chill."

Dad and his cold washrag would seek out my feet that were hiding between the sheets and covers at the end of the bed. I'd tuck, roll, and squeal. We'd laugh.

There is just no way you can keep your feet completely tucked under the covers when Mr. Washcloth is around. Like a camel's nose under the edge of a tent, it was only

iT'S HARD TO GET UP iN THE MORNiNG

—Especially If You're a Teenager

Everyone knows how hard it is to get teenagers up in the morning, but it is not all their fault. Until age eleven or twelve, children have little trouble going to sleep at a decent hour.

However, the onset of puberty affects the sleep cycle, lengthening it from the normal twenty-four-hour cycle to a twenty-five or twenty-six-hour cycle. Teenagers' internal clocks, now flooded with hormones, tell them to go to bed an hour or two later each night. No wonder they're out of sync with the rest of us![18]

a matter of time before our game of "hide and feet" ended with me wide-awake and cold footed. Our opening ritual of the day was complete.

Morning rituals often become sacred memories. Last year, Dad's sister-in-law—my Aunt Judy—passed away. As we reminisced about her life, I said, "We ought to sing 'Wake Up Jacob' in honor of Aunt Judy." Everyone groaned and then smiled at the memory of Judy singing that awful song as she greeted the morning and each and every one of us whenever we spent the night with the Baileys.

Wake up Jacob days a breakin',
beans in the pot and bacon's baking.
Tra la la la boom de ay
Tra la la la boom de ay.

It could be the first time those words ever brought a tear *and* a smile to those who heard them. I discovered we had several different versions of the lyrics for that song.

It's hard to catch all the words when you're trying to snatch a few extra winks.

Dad and Aunt Judy loved mornings, even if the rest of us didn't share their enthusiasm at the time. My body now wakes me at 6 A.M. every morning—guess it comes with growing old. Still, I see it as a blessing, for morning is now my favorite time of the day to think, write, and pray.

I don't suppose I'll ever be awakened to "Wake Up, Jacob" again, and no one has greeted me in the morning with a cold washrag in a long time. But I'm still warmed by the memories of those cold morning rituals. Wonder how my wife, Luci, would respond to old Mr. Washcloth? I suspect there are some things better left a mystery.

WHAT MY DAD TAUGHT ME

How you greet the day has a lot to do with how you connect with others throughout the day.

> *Early to bed, early to rise, makes a man healthy, wealth, and wise—especially if he has good genes, a substantial inheritance, and nothing much happens after nine o'clock at night.*

> —Gary Stanley

HUGS

ugging is a lost art. Some hugs are mechanical rituals with all the warmth of a Hollywood air kiss bestowed on a lifelong rival, an obligatory duty dictated by custom and condescension. Some people hug too hard, with a crushing, dominant sort of hug—a controlling hug. That sort of hug tends to bruise the spirit, freeze the heart, and tighten the muscles in your back.

Some hugs are too tentative. The hugger seems afraid to touch you, and you begin to wonder if you should have used more deodorant. Other hugs are simply out of sync. They catch you off guard and raise all sorts of questions that muddy the relationship. And then there are "vampire hugs"—full of need, draining, giving nothing in return.

A healthy hug shouldn't be taken for granted.

The right kind of hug lifts your burdens for a moment, giving you a chance to catch your breath and let down your guard. A safe, embracing hug grants you permission to surrender personal space, abandon isolation, and connect.

Your skin is the largest sense organ in your body (about 12 percent of your total body weight) and has a network of 5 million sensory cells and responders that collectively grant the gift of touch. No wonder there have been dozens of studies on the benefits of hugging. According to Virginia Satir, "We need four hugs for survival. We need eight hugs a day for maintenance. We need twelve hugs a day for growth." Another study says that husbands who hug their wives on a regular basis tend to live three years longer and have fewer heart problems than those who don't. Hugs can be a matter of life and death.

My dad was a hugger. A gentle giant, he could put his arm around you and that simple act made the world a safer place. He always sensed when I needed to be enfolded in his arms—to know that I was safe and loved, that I belonged. He hugged me all the time.

Mom wasn't much of a hugger. My folks didn't fit the norm. His was the tender heart. Her heart was more carefully kept. Oh, she had a playful heart, taught dance, and was gifted in the bodily art of movement and grace. But she didn't understand the ways of hugging at the level Dad did. Her daddy died during the Influenza Epidemic of 1919; she was two years old at the time (Aunt Judy was four, and Uncle John was only six days old). Daddy hugs aren't a part of her conscious memory. At eighty-two, she's still learning how to translate all the love inside her into the embrace of a hug.

Dad initiated most of the hugs in our home.

I remember one day when Mom came home from work tired and frustrated. She was a first-grade teacher, and a room full of six-year-olds had "done her in." It was one of those days when she'd had no opportunity to get rid of the toxin of prolonged aggravation—being nibbled to death by ducks. Mom banged the cabinet doors and started to simmer something on the stove. Several things were coming to a rolling boil in the kitchen that afternoon.

Time to get out of the way, I thought. Time to head downstairs and catch a bit of television on the black-and-white portable.

Dad followed me downstairs and stood in the doorway. "Looks

WHAT'S IN A TOUCH

Emperor Frederick II could have been the greatest emperor Germany had ever known. He had a brilliant intellect and a level of curiosity unknown in the thirteenth century. He was a brave and courageous leader. But he was also cruel. He lacked a spiritual and moral compass.

Frederick was curious about the acquisition of language. Was the language one spoke a matter of biology, handed down by the parents? Was it a matter of environment? Or did one simply learn what one heard? Was it possible that a child raised in isolation would grow up naturally speaking Hebrew, Greek, or even Latin?

Mothers lost their babies to Frederick's experiments. The babies were fed but never held or spoken to. They all died. Salimbene, the chronicler of those times, wrote in 1248, "They could not live without caressing."[19]

like thirty first graders have taken a toll on Mom today. I suspect we wouldn't have fared any better. Let's give her a hug!"

Dad was much more hopeful than I that a hug would help, so we marched upstairs to embrace a mother who didn't want to be embraced at that particular moment. He stepped into her personal space and unlocked the chains around her tense heart. To Mom's credit, she didn't bolt and bar the walls erected around her. She let Dad in, and the cares of the day began to dissipate like a static charge running down a grounding wire. It wasn't long before the three of us were in a group hug in the middle of the kitchen with our dog Waddles dancing around our feet.

It's been said that the best way to love a child is to love the child's mother. That day in the kitchen I was invited into a relationship that existed before I was born and that didn't depend on me. Of all the hugs I ever saw or got, the ones Dad gave Mom have meant the most.

WHAT MY DAD TAUGHT ME

We all long to be invited into a loving relationship that doesn't depend on us.

> "To have and to hold from this day forward" isn't just a license to hug—it's a promise to be kept.
>
> —Gary Stanley

A TEACHABLE HEART BEGINS IN THE TEACHER

SECTION iii

SPECKS, LOGS, AND TEACHERS

The greatest teacher who has ever lived once remarked, "The student, after he has been fully trained, will be like his teacher." He said this immediately before observing that you have to take the log out of your own eye before you can help anyone else get the speck out of his or her eye.

Makes a lot of sense—it isn't the content of the class that makes all the difference; it's the content of the teacher.

When the student falls asleep in class, there's only one thing to do: Get a sharp stick and poke the teacher.[20]

MY FiRST
TREE HOUSE

One year I thought it would be a good idea to build a tree house, a refuge in the sky. We'd just moved, so I had few playmates at the moment. Just down the street was the perfect tree. It was tall and leafy, with a sturdy looking Y-shaped limb ten feet off the ground, and it was close to the curb so I could watch the cars go by, unseen, from my perch. Three doors down, it was far enough from my house that parental permission wasn't necessary. Destiny!

I grabbed a few nails, a hammer, and some scrap lumber and started nailing the "stairs" leading to my future tree house onto the trunk of the tree. I was working on the third step when the woman who happened to live in the house directly behind the tree came out to see who was taking over her tree. What she found was an enthusiastic seven-year-old with big dreams.

She was very kind. She explained that all those nail holes I was making were an open invitation to every bug in town to come and eat her tree. I caught the emphasis on "her" and realized that my dream house was only that—a dream. I pulled the boards out of the tree under her watchful eye and was sent home.

My face burned with embarrassment. I didn't know the rules, but I was a trespasser all the same. No building permit . . . no zoning rights . . . no nothin'. All I had to show for my efforts were three boards with four twisted nails in the middle of each. I tried not to cry.

I don't remember mentioning my failed building project. Perhaps our neighbor told my folks. Either way, Dad decided that what we needed in the backyard was a tree house. And this was not to be just any old tree house.

He set up his draftsman's desk, got out his plastic orange triangles and drafting paper, adjusted his elbowed desk light, and set about to design the kind of tree house you could only dream about. A day or two later, a truck showed up at our house and dumped a sizable load of lumber—two-by-fours, half-inch plywood, a box of sixteen-penny nails, and a fistful of eight-inch bolts and nuts. I began to think we might rent out our house and all live in the tree!

This was the first real building project I'd ever worked on with my dad. Up to that point, my tools were toys, and my projects all came in a box or a round cardboard

Lincoln Log tube. But that summer I began to learn the rules of carpentry:

- "Think your project through before you start."
- "Measure twice, cut once—measure once, cut twice."
- "A workman is only as good as his tools."
- "Put things away at the end of the day."
- "Cut against the grain and never try to muscle your way through a piece of wood, especially with a Skilsaw."

And with that advice, Dad would rip a two-by-four or piece of plywood, and I would put my fingers in my ears against the scream of the saw.

A simple nail provides a host of lessons. There is a practiced art to planting a nail so the head is just below the surface with only a slight dimple marking the wood. Most of my attempts resulted in a bent nail with half a dozen gouges in the surrounding area. I discovered that the best way to put a nail through a knothole is to drill the nail hole first. Pulling nails is an art as well. I think that was the first time Dad ever brought up Archimedes and his fulcrum—"Give me a fixed point and a long enough fulcrum, and I can move the world." Then Dad turned his hammer to the side and pulled a stubborn nail out of the wood.

We built a large square base around the trunk of our backyard tree about six feet off the ground. I think Dad managed the whole thing without ever putting a nail through bark. Instead he bolted two double-thick wooden collars tightly around the trunk, one six feet up and the other about three feet off the ground. Then he rested the platform on one and ran braces down from the corners to the lower collar. Our tree house wasn't going anywhere.

Eventually a trap door, complete with a wooden ladder that could be hoisted inside in case of enemy attack, was set in the floor. Walls, windows, and roof were soon in place, and with Mom's help, it soon had all the comforts of home.

We lived in that Little Rock, Arkansas, house for just under a year. Dad always meant to move on to Boulder, Colorado, after he helped Uncle Wig get started in the building business. He enjoyed telling folks, "We wanted to make a big change, and so we moved from Little Rock to Boulder."

The year was 1957. "Jail House Rock" was a hit. I discovered that you never want to run over a turtle with the lawn mower, and Waddles, the pup we got at the beginning of the year, was about to have a litter of pups of her own. It was also the year of the tree house. I've never seen another tree house that was so grand—no, that's not true. The Swiss Family Robinson

THE TREE HOUSE OF TREE HOUSES

You really could live in the Swiss Family Robinson Tree House at Disneyland. It has running water that is supplied by a system of bamboo buckets at the rate of 200 gallons per hour. But there are some down sides, like a lot of steps (137 to be exact). Finding the right location to put it could also be a problem—it is 70 feet tall, 80 feet wide, and weighs 150 tons! But the biggest challenge is likely to be the 300,000 vinyl leaves that have to be changed by hand four times a year to reflect the change of seasons.[21]

Tree House at Disneyland is grander, but then you can't pull up the ladder in case of enemy attacks.

I expect that tree house is long gone. I wonder if any other little boys enjoyed my father's labor of love. For me, I can't drive a nail or cut a piece of wood without hearing somewhere in the background my father's voice and instruction. I suppose everything I've built since then has his mark on it.

WHAT MY DAD TAUGHT ME

The best kind of building is the "building into" kind.

*If you think about it, all of
creation is a Father/Son project.*

THE FiNER POiNTS OF THE GAME

i went to a major league ball game the other day with friends. Our team won. Sitting there in the stands watching the repetitive themes that accompany all ball games, taking in the smells and sounds, I remembered another time long ago.

Dad started taking me to ball games as soon as I was big enough to go. He built some apartment buildings, and several of the minor league players from the local AA League rented from him.

Because we knew some of the players, we got to sit directly behind the home dugout. They had a bat boy on the field, but I was the concession stands boy in the bleachers. I fetched hot dogs and drinks for the team, and they rewarded me with broken bats and retired baseballs. What a game!

It was there on the bleachers that Dad taught me the finer points of the game, like a count of two balls, two strikes, and two outs is called "ducks on a pond." (I recently learned that ducks on a pond really refer to the runners in scoring position but 2 2 2 does look a bit like a bunch of ducks). I also learned the verbal part of the game. Dad gave a running commentary on strikes and balls, close calls at the plate, and when to call for a sacrifice fly or lay down a bunt.

One evening Dad was kibitzing during a particularly difficult game. The home team was behind, and the fans were all over one of the regular umpires, a friend of Dad's. In a moment of deep frustration, the ump walked over to Dad and said, "G. L., one more word out of you, and I'm gonna make you ump this game!" Dad was so taken back, he held up both hands in mock surrender, "Have I told you what a wonderful job you're doing?" And with that, the ump put his facemask back on and marched back to home plate.

Dad bought me a glove and showed me how to break it in by oiling it and wrapping it around a ball. We played catch in the backyard. He threw grounders, and I silently repeated his advice to myself, *Get your body in front of the ball; don't just stick out your glove in hopes of fielding it.* That way, if I missed the ball with my glove, I still stopped it with my body. I stopped a lot of balls with my body (sort of a specialty of mine).

Dad taught me to choke up on the bat, step into my swing, and "watch the ball hit the bat." Ever notice that you can't actually watch a speeding ball hit a swinging bat?

Seems to me his verbal game was a lot better than his actual game. But he loved baseball, and I was just like him.

I played Little League for the Red Owl Supermarket team. I use the word "play" loosely. My first season, I carried a .500 batting average for the first half of the season; I only got up to bat three times (a walk, a single, and a ground out). Mostly I sat on the bench or stood in right field long after the critical moments of the game had passed.

Worse still, when the coach passed out the uniforms one season, he came up one pair of maroon baseball socks short. Every game I endured the heckling of the other team as the only one who had to play in regular white socks. I'd like to think this was the major reason for my entirely forgettable athletic

THE NUMBER FIVE ON JOE'S BACK

Joe Dimaggio was one of the greatest right hand hitters baseball has ever known. But he went into a batting slump in the middle of his career. He couldn't have bought a hit. His wife sat in the same box seat every game day and watched Joe swing away. He went 0 for 42 at bats. He couldn't figure out what he was doing wrong. Joe went out early for batting practice and worked until his hands were like hamburger meat. Hendricks, the batting coach, worked endlessly with him. Nothing helped.

Finally, after going 0 for 4 in a game, he went home and lay in bed wondering if he could still play. His wife turned to him and said, "I don't know if it makes any difference or not, but I notice that after you swing, I don't see the number five on your uniform the same way I did in the first part of the season."

Joe jumped out of bed (it was the middle of the night) and went to the ballpark. He got the groundskeeper out of bed and had him turn on the lights. To his wife he said, "Sit in your box seat. I'm going to hit, and you watch me until you see the number five like you did before." Joe swung and swung until she finally said, "That's it!" Then he swung and swung some more until he got it right. The next night Joe Dimaggio started his 56-game hitting streak. It is a major league record that still stands.[22]

career, but it probably had more to do with my average ability and tendency to approach the game mentally rather than physically. Why does it take so long to mature physically? Throughout my athletic career, I was good enough to make most teams but seldom good enough to play regularly.

Three knee surgeries and a fifty-year-old body have curtailed much of my interest in playing any serious ball. But give me a summer night at the local park with the kids on the field and their parents in the stands, and I'll mistakenly point out the "ducks on the pond," cheer each play, and yell at the ump for old-time's sake.

WHAT MY DAD TAUGHT ME

Never let a little thing like not being good at something keep you from enjoying it.

> *Eighty percent of the men in this country*
> *think they are above average athletically.*

WORKING FOR DAD

When I was five years old, my job was to water the trees around our house. We're not talking about just a couple of trees—we're talking dozens of young saplings. This was a new house, and Dad believed in foliage. I dragged the hose, actually three hoses fastened together, around the back forty, filling the earthen bowl at the base of each tree twice a day. I also got to repair any breaks in the circular dams around the trees with a shovel as big as me. I made ten cents an hour—good money back then, but muddy.

At the age of nine, I was given the opportunity to pull dandelions out of our front yard. Dad agreed to pay me a quarter for every grocery bag full of weeds I collected. Living across the street from a field, we never lacked for weeds. The only problem was that a full sack of fresh weeds tends to shrink over time, and a paper bag that was full at noon was only about two-thirds full by five o'clock.

"This bag doesn't look rightly full," Dad would tease. "Seems like twenty cents would be about right." I'd wade right in with how it was a full bag earlier in the day and eventually got the full twenty-five cents for each bag of weeds regardless of shrinkage.

The summer of my tenth year, I was the bus boy at the Bar-B-Quick, a short-lived lunch spot on the corner of Broadway and Pearl. It was my dad's one and only attempt at becoming a restaurateur. I worked a two-hour shift on Saturdays and once (and only once) got a quarter tip to supplement my fifty cents an hour wage.

The next year Dad started a subdivision east of Boulder, and I eventually graduated from work-site pickup guy to bathroom tile man. I was about to make the transition from unskilled to skilled labor. This was huge!

Dad showed me the finer points of tile work as we worked together. After he showed me how to score a tile and break it along the score, we checked the sheet rock to make sure there were no nails sticking up that would interfere with a smooth layer of tile. Then we measured (twice) to see if we'd have to cut a row of tile to come out even, and if so, where we wanted to cut. We popped chalk lines to help us keep the rows straight and figured out where we wanted to start (usually a corner).

Next we took turns spreading the black adhesive on the wall with a saw-tooth trowel, taking pains to keep it even (never spread more than you can cover in thirty minutes). After all that, it was time to place the first tile, check its position (twice) and firmly press it into place. After a few rows, Dad left me on my own and went to check on the rest of the building crew.

Two or three rows later, Dad popped his head into the bathroom. "How are you doing? Any problems or questions? No? You're doing a good job, Gary."

The next time he checked on me, he just stood at the door and watched. After a moment, he said, "Gary, let's get some air."

Huh? Dad's voice had an odd quality to it. I felt a little funny, and each motion seem-ed to blur into the next. He extended a hand and led me out of the bathroom. "Meet me out front," he said. "I have a quick errand to run, and then we'll see how everyone else is doing."

Dad soon joined me out front, and we walked around the construction site. I didn't think anything of it at the time. We walked together all the

THE WORKING CONCLUSIONS OF STUDS TERKEL

Studs Terkel! Isn't that a great name? You can sand wood with a name like that. Terkel traveled all around the country interviewing hundreds of folks about their occupations and reached some interesting conclusions.

"I think most of us are looking for a calling, not a job," he says. "Most of us have jobs that are too small for our spirits. Jobs are not big enough for people.

"[Life] is a search for daily meaning as well as daily bread, for recognition as well as cause, for astonishment rather than torpor; in short for a sort of a life rather than a Monday through Friday sort of dying."[23]

time. After about fifteen minutes, he looked me in the eye and said, "Well, it's about time we get back to work." And with that, we headed back to my unfinished project.

The bathroom had a new addition since we'd left. A large box fan was blowing fresh air into my cubicle. It wasn't all that hot out, and the fan was kind of noisy, but Dad insisted it was a good idea. I never gave it another thought until years later.

I was attending classes at the University of Colorado in the '60s. Professors occasionally treated us to guest lectures that ranged in topic from diatribes for the Students for a More Democratic Society (SDS) to how to get high on a banana peel (Psyche-Delicatessen 101). On one such occasion, I found myself in a lecture hall that was large, dark, and packed. As the lecturer droned on, and the sweet, sticky smell of marijuana wafted through the room, I found my thoughts drifting. *I need some fresh air; a good box fan by the window would do the trick. Hmmm. The fumes of bathroom tile adhesive must be hallucinogenic! And here I thought this class was going to be a complete waste of time.*

What My Dad Taught Me

There are some things you don't need an explanation for at any age.

> *Manual labor to my father was not only good and*
> *decent for its own sake but, as he was given*
> *to saying, it straightened out one's thoughts.*
>
> —Mary Ellen Chase

My First Car and a Better Mousetrap

Remember where you first learned to drive? Perhaps you sat in your daddy's lap and "helped" him steer the car or had the privilege of backing the car down the driveway. Or maybe you lived close to a go-cart track! I can go you one better—my dad built my first car.

The local five-and-dime store (where I threw my one and only temper tantrum) sponsored a drawing for a miniature, fiberglass, electric sports car. It was slick, sleek, and shiny. The doors opened, the horn honked, the headlights beamed, and you could actually drive it! Every kid in the neighborhood entered the drawing and checked out the dream prize every chance they got. The eventual winner lived just a block or two away from us. I remember seeing him driving his motorized winnings down our street—lucky guy.

You can either wait for good fortune to come your way, or you can make some of your own. Dad was of the second opinion. He loved to quote Ralph Waldo Emerson who said, "Build a better mousetrap, and the world will beat a path to your door." He wasn't the least bit shy about trying his hand at building one of those better "mousetraps." His inventions ranged from a do-it-yourself, plywood sauna kit to a fiberglass popcorn-dispensing machine (one sat in the lobby of the Paramount Theater for years—the popcorn dispenser, not the sauna).

Dad found an old electric motor, a battery, a battery charger, and enough wood, wire, and wheels to build his one and only son a homemade go-cart of his own.

If you were looking for beauty, dependability, and maintenance-free performance, you might as well look somewhere else. But if you were in the market for functionality, here it was. My two-by-four wooden go-cart full of nuts and bolts, wires and cables, and four (almost matching) wheels was actually a tad faster than the dawdling fiberglass sports car from the five-and-dime drawing. Of course it didn't have doors that opened or a nice paint job, but it was a winner (at least for the few minutes that the battery held a full charge). I also pushed it home on several occasions when the battery died and waited an eternity for it to recharge—my first car.

I'm not sure how much I learned about driving, since most of it was on a sidewalk at speeds just under that of a brisk walk. But I sure learned a lot about maintenance, patience, and the ingenuity needed to position a block of wood against the frame and motor so that the fan belt that doubled as the drive chain actually did its job rather than burning up.

The world never beat a path to Dad's door to buy one of his "better mousetraps." But he did build something that mixed enough success and challenge to keep *me* coming back to him to celebrate my victories and get pointers on how to keep it running. Not sure you can get any more successful than that.

THE TUCKER TORPEDO

Few people know more about the challenge of building a car from the ground up than Preston Thomas Tucker (1903-1956). In the 1940s Tucker sold franchises across the country for his "car of the future." His Tucker Torpedo pioneered a number of automotive features that would later become standard. It had the first sealed cooling system, a safety glass windshield that popped out on impact, a cushion-edged dashboard, and an engine that would take it from zero to sixty in ten seconds.

Tucker raised millions of dollars in his attempt to break into the mass car market. He took on the "Big Three"—Ford, General Motors, and Chrysler—and they took him on. He soon found himself mired in bureaucratic red tape and on trial for fraud and a host of related charges. Though he was later cleared of all charges, only fifty-one Tucker Torpedoes were ever built (forty-seven are still around). Each one originally cost $2,450; today you would need between $250,000 and $500,000 to buy one—if you could find someone willing to part with it.[24]

WHAT MY DAD TAUGHT ME

Better the well-worn path of a son to your door than the whole world at your gate.

> *Build a better mousetrap, and the world will beat a path to your door—provided you get the proper licenses, government approvals, advertising strategy, financial backing, and catch the competition asleep.*
>
> —Gary Stanley
> *(unless it turns out James Thurber made this addition to Emerson's quote and I forgot he did)*

JACKPOT

When I was nine, we stopped by Las Vegas on our way to the West Coast. The millions of lights on the downtown strip and giant, neon-waving cowboy turned night into day. The gamblers fed coins into one-armed bandits, and the clink of coins hitting the pay-out tray was a siren's song pulling me closer to the shores of chance. Who wouldn't want to participate in such an enticing environment?

We were standing in front of one of the casinos. The slot machines all but spilled out onto the sidewalk as fellow tourists passed by. Tantalizingly close but forbidden territory—in those days kids weren't allowed in the gambling areas.

Dad had probably planned his object lesson miles before we reached Las Vegas. "Son, this whole place is built on the myth that you can beat the odds. See that sign over there that says the slots pay out 97 percent of the time? Sounds like you have a 97 percent chance of winning, doesn't it? But what it really means is that for every dollar you feed into one of their slot machines you'll only get 97 cents back."

As Dad warmed to his statistical lesson, I continued to take in all the sights and sounds. It didn't seem fair that kids couldn't wander around the gambling tables and machines. The whole place looked more like a playground than some adult business.

"To prove my point, Gary, I'm going to feed a dollar's worth of nickels into this slot machine next to the sidewalk. I want you to watch. I'll probably get a few nickels back from time to time just to entice me to keep on playing. But it won't be long before our dollar is gone." Dad put his first nickel into the machine and pulled the lever. Tumblers whirled and clicked

THE NOT SO HIDDEN COST

Who hasn't dreamed of hitting the jackpot and buying a new car and taking the vacation of a lifetime? Not all that long ago, Nevada was the only place you could legally play the slots or poker, and New Hampshire had the only legal lottery.

By 1999, thirty-seven states had lotteries, and gambling was legal in some form in all but three states (Utah, Tennessee, and Hawaii). Collectively, we Americans now spend more on gambling than we do on movies. Gross revenues for gambling exceeded fifty billion dollars in 1999.

However, the cost to society is even greater. A University of Illinois study found that the social and criminal cost to states is three times as high as the profits gained from gambling. Between fifteen and twenty million of us are now in danger of becoming problem gamblers.[25]

one at a time into place. No lights went off. No bells rang, signaling a winner. Dad smiled and put in another nickel.

Dad was about thirty-five cents in the hole when his object lesson went south. All of a sudden, the slot he was feeding lit up and began to disgorge a mountain of nickels! We were winners!

"Dad! We ought to move here and just play the slots! Money will never be a problem again!"

Dad shook his head and laughed. Go figure. He didn't want to spend the time it would take to put all those nickels back in the machine, so he quit while he was still ahead. I got to pocket his jackpot—two and a half rolls of nickels totaling $2.50. His failed object lesson led to many future discussions on probability and statistics and the wise use of money.

Guess you could say he eventually made his point since gambling has held little attraction for me—too well prepared to ever fall for the myth of beating the house. Though I must confess to occasionally returning the Reader's Digest Sweepstakes form just to give God the chance to be gracious if He so chooses. I don't think Dad would mind, knowing I've figured out that the price of the stamp against the odds of winning the grand prize still makes it a sucker bet.

WHAT MY DAD TAUGHT ME
A single incident seldom tells the whole story.

The best throw of the dice is to throw them away.
—Austin O'Mallet

FROM SPARROW TO BLUEBIRD ON A GRAPEVINE

n third grade the "Bluebirds" were the top readers. The "Sparrows" were at the bottom of the reading totem pole. I was a Sparrow. Reading out loud in class was only slightly less embarrassing than participating in class spelling contests.

Our family had picked up and moved to three different states during my first three years in school. Apparently, I'd transferred schools once too often and missed a critical moment when the letters should have come together into words. So I ended up reading out loud to a grandmotherly former teacher for two afternoons a week. I looked forward to those afternoons with all the excitement I mustered to face my piano lessons. (You can read about that in the next chapter.)

My remedial reading teacher picked the classic *Farmer Boy*, a slow, plodding book to my way of thinking, for our afternoon reading sessions. I was about to be doomed to Sparrow status for the rest of my life due to someone else's taste in literature!

One day Dad picked up my book, read a few pages, and said, "Gary, this weekend I'm going to buy you the book that was my favorite when I was growing up. It is full of adventures and lore and survival techniques." He wouldn't tell me the name of this mythical wonder. But throughout the week, he salted my appetite for this book of heroic adventures.

The weekend finally arrived, and we drove down to Denver and the most wonderful department store in all of Colorado, May D & F. Its slanting roof, ice skating rink, and Christmas windows were a magnet to me. In a far corner of that store was an immense section of dark, highly polished shelves that reached far overhead and were filled with hardback books. High up on one of those shelves was the book that would change me from a Sparrow to a Bluebird—the first of over ninety books by the same author. I eventually read just about all of them.

Hard to keep your eye from drifting down the page to see the title, isn't it? I hesitate to tell you. If you haven't actually read it, you can't possibly understand what lies between the covers. Today it would be considered college-level reading.

Here are the opening lines of that incredible book:

I had this tale from one who had no right to tell it to me, or to any other. I may credit the seductive influence of an old vintage upon the narrator for the beginning of it, and my own skeptical incredulity during the days that followed for the balance of the strange tale.

When my convivial host discovered that he had told me so much, and that I was prone to doubtfulness, his foolish pride assumed the task the old vintage had commenced, and so he unearthed written evidence in the form of musty manuscript, and dry official records of the British Colonial Office to support many of the salient features of his remarkable narrative.

I do not say the story is true, for I did not witness the happenings which it portrays, but the fact that in the telling of it to you I have taken fictitious names for the principal characters quite sufficiently

THE TARZAN YOU'VE NEVER SEEN ON THE SILVER SCREEN

The Tarzan you meet between the covers of some thirty books written by Edgar Rice Burroughs never said, "Me Tarzan. You Jane." His son's name was "Korak," not "Boy," and his home was a ranch, not a tree house. He was familiar with many of the great cities of Europe and America, fluent in numerous languages, and served as a colonel in the Royal Air Force during WWII.

evidences the sincerity of my own belief that it *may* be true.[26]

It took me nine months to digest that book the first time. But three things kept me at it—a marvelous story, the knowledge that my father saw in it something that could turn me from a Sparrow into a Bluebird, and the fact that we did it together.

President Ronald Reagan was once asked for a list of the books that shaped his life. Near the top of that list was the book that still sits on my shelf, a first edition hardback of *Tarzan of the Apes* by Edgar Rice Burroughs— the very book Dad bought for me all those years ago when all I could see in reading was a lifetime of drudgery.

WHAT MY DAD TAUGHT ME

It takes a long time to acquire a skill, but, once acquired, it gives a good return for a long time to come.

A truly great book should be read in youth,
again in maturity, and once more in old age.

—*Robertson Davies*

MUSICALLY CHALLENGED

Dad was the original Johnny One Note. When he sang in church, the melody took a back seat, fell off the apple cart, landed flatter than a fritter, and was murdered and buried in an unmarked grave.

You might think that because Dad was a poor singer, it would have caused him to be more of a meditative worshipper during the hymns. You'd be wrong. He had a musical soul but not one ounce of talent.

He belted out the words, and he knew every one of them. Anyone sitting within five pews of Dad was going to have a hard time staying with the music. It was the musical equivalent of trying to rub your stomach and pat your head at the same time. Regulars were used to it; they either learned to sing against the dissonance or move.

Visitors had a harder time. By the end of the first verse, they usually gave up and with puzzled expressions watched Dad's enthusiastic performance.

With head thrown back and eyes shut, Dad was loud, articulate, and nowhere near the key everyone else was singing in. He loved to quote the bit in Psalm 66 about "making a joyful noise." He reminded folks that the Bible never mentions singing on key.

Standing next to him in church every Sunday didn't improve my own attempts at singing. I probably should have been embarrassed by his singular lack of talent that was put on display each and every week. But I guess I was too busy trying to figure out how to sing the songs myself to be particularly worried about the melody. Besides, everyone loved Dad's enthusiasm too much for me to be embarrassed by him.

Dad didn't limit his musical impulses to church. He hardly ever got into the car but that he broke into song. Down the road we went, singing all the great classics at the top of our lungs—"Picking Up Paw Paws, Puttin' Em in Your Pocket," "Clementine" (all verses), "She'll Be Coming around the Mountain," and "Crawdad Hole."

Mom was more musically inclined than Dad, although that's not saying much. She used to talk about practicing her piano lessons on a long board that had all the black and white keys painted on it. Her family couldn't afford a real piano, so she moved her fingers and imagined what the music would sound like. Must have been a bit like playing air guitar—I think Dad might have been pretty good on Mom's painted keyboard.

In any event, by the time I arrived in the Stanley household, Mom had realized her dream of having a real piano, and there was a Betsy Ross spinet in the living room that nobody could play. It was decided that I was to be the family musician. Piano lessons commenced when I was five and didn't stop until I was twelve.

Three times a week I dutifully sat on the piano bench, pounded a few keys, and watched the clock. "Spinning Wheel" came and went as did hundreds of musical works for which I had little use. I suspect they all sounded the same to Dad; the way I played they probably sounded the same to everyone. Once a week, Mom or Dad would haul me off to my piano lesson and pick me up half an hour later none the worse . . . or better.

In third grade I was introduced to the Whittier Grade-School Band. Because I was all arms and legs, it was deemed that I would be a trombone player. You needed long arms to reach seventh position and that turned out to be my only natural advantage for playing the blasted thing. The kid who always sat one chair in front of me couldn't reach seventh position and had to use a string tied to his slide and wrist to sling his instrument to reach that elusive position. For all that, he still played rings around me and my easy stretch to seventh.

The pinnacle of my trombone talent reared its head one afternoon when the bandleader stepped out for a few minutes during practice, leaving us to our own devices. I soon discovered that a trombone slide (minus the mouthpiece and outer slide) is an ideal instrument for delivering spitballs. It was the one and only time I truly mastered my dinged up old Reynolds. Ah, the improvisation! The accuracy! The breath control! A virtuoso performance that gave new meaning to the spit valve—move over Glenn Miller!

I eventually took up the guitar and reached the point where a few distracted individuals found my meager ability mildly interesting.

Dad's musical modeling didn't accomplish much if measured on the scale of well-played etudes and arpeggios. His love of music didn't propagate itself through his genes, but

IF YOU PRACTICE BADLY, YOU WILL PLAY BADLY VERY WELL

"If we catch a very young, wild nightingale in the spring and put a good-voiced nightingale beside it for about thirty days, the throat of the baby nightingale changes so that it will be able to sing like its teacher.... If we use a gramophone to train a nightingale, the bird will sing accordingly—even imitating the sound of the needle going over the surface of the record. Almost the same may be said of human beings. Children listen to the pronouncing of words by their parents and their vocal chords adjust themselves physiologically to make the same kind of pronunciation as their parents.... If a nightingale that sings poorly is kept close to a young nightingale for some time, the young bird will learn to sing poorly."[27]

it did get passed down through his soul. I still love to hold forth with a good song, even if I can't reach all the high notes or keep a steady beat. Choirs and musicals have long been a part of my life—even married a classical musician and now know the difference between medieval, renaissance, baroque, classical, romantic, and twentieth-century music.

I doubt that Dad ever learned the finer points of musical history or theory. He wouldn't have known the difference between a Gregorian chant and Chopin's "Polonaise." He had no ear for it. But he did have a melody playing deep inside where it counts.

Most people are more concerned about singing the right notes than enjoying the music. Most people shy away from the things they have no talent for. Most people are more afraid of looking foolish than joining in. Most people don't see the need of passing along the things they never had. Dad wasn't "most people."

WHAT MY DAD TAUGHT ME

If it's worth doing but you can't do it well, do it anyway with all your heart.

> *The average person goes to his grave*
> *with his music still in him.*
>
> —Oliver Wendell Holmes

PLAYING AT MY LEVEL

I've played a lot of Ping-Pong in my time—even won a tournament once in grad school. But one person I could never beat was my dad.

We had an empty basement room in our home, just the place to erect a Ping-Pong table. Not one of those store-bought jobs, this was a real Ping-Pong table made of plywood, sawhorses, and paint. And in at least one major windstorm, it also served as a temporary shutter for a big west-facing window that had blown out during the night.

Dad taught me how to hold the paddle western style and reverse grip, put a spin on the ball, slam, undercut, and short hop. We shoved the table against the sheetrock, and I played against the wall perfecting my rhythm and eye. Dad made a contest of every game; he played at my level. In the beginning our goal was to see how many times we could hit the ball back and forth over the net. He sent back easy lobs with no spin right in the middle of the table. As I progressed, so did he.

After awhile he began to play me left-handed, putting more pace on the ball. Eventually we got to the point where he had to shift back to his right hand to win. We used every trick in the book in our daily Ping-Pong campaigns. We stretched the confines of the room as we moved farther and farther from the table to retrieve overhand smashes and wicked slices. And still he won— every game.

No matter how far ahead I was or how close I'd get to that elusive twenty-one, he always found a way to pull out every game. We played from the time I was ten until I was almost thirteen, and though my game greatly improved, it was never enough to best Dad.

I still remember venting my frustration one day. "Why can't you let me win at least one game!"

"If I let you win, would it really mean anything?" Dad asked. "One day, in the not too distant future, you'll be my equal, and later you'll be my better. Do you really want me to 'give' you a game rather than winning it outright?"

Well, when he put it that way, of course I didn't want him to forfeit a game to my ego. I wanted to know I was good enough to honestly beat him. And so I continued to lose to my dad, but losing took on a different definition—each loss was a step toward winning. I began to realize that Dad's goal wasn't to frustrate me but rather to lay a winning foundation.

What is easily attained is seldom valued. Winning a "gimme" doesn't make you a winner. I revisited that lesson often during my doctoral days—all seven years, eleven months, twenty-one days, and eleven hours of them. Many times I thought, *You've passed all the classes and survived the qualifying exams, now all that's left is an acceptable dissertation. Don't I already know enough for them to just give me the Ph.D.?* But then I'd think, *No, they don't give these things away; it is in the finishing of the entire course that one is a "doctor." It wouldn't mean much if it wasn't earned fair and square.* So I would go back and "lose" some more, knowing that each loss was a step toward winning.

Wish you could have been there, Dad, to see me earn my degree. Perhaps we

AS THE BALL BOUNCES

As far as anyone knows, British army officers stationed in India in the early 1880s were the first to play table tennis. They used a row of books set in the middle of a good-sized table for the net, the lids off cigar boxes for paddles, and rounded wine corks as balls.

By the 1890s the game had spread to England. An Englishman named James Gibb bought some small hollow celluloid balls he saw on his visit to America in 1900 and began playing table tennis with them back home. He is credited as the first to call them Ping-Pong balls because of the sound they made, and the name stuck. In 1902 wooden paddles with pebbled rubber surfaces were invented, and the first world championship was held in London in 1927.

Ping-Pong became an Olympic sport in 1988, but it is officially called table tennis because "Ping-Pong" is a registered trademark owned by Parker Brothers.[28]

could have celebrated with a Ping-Pong game. I think I might be able to take you now. And like the degree, it would mean something.

Over the years I've tried to play Ping-Pong at the level of my opponent. I'm not a bad left-handed player, and it's more fun to play a close game than a lopsided one. Still, I've seldom lost a game to someone whose level I was trying to match—it wouldn't mean much now, would it? The one notable exception is Luci. In all of our married life, she won just one game of Ping-Pong. Of course, that's the one we still celebrate. She bested me, and it meant something—still does.

WHAT MY DAD TAUGHT ME

Winning isn't a momentary effort but rather a long, well-coached preparation.

> *If anyone competes as an athlete, he does not win the prize unless he competes according to the rules.*
>
> 2 Timothy 2:5

THE DOUBLE-CLUTCH TRACTOR AND THE PICKUP TRUCK

The little tractor didn't actually work when Dad got it. That was part of its charm. Who wants to drive something that asks almost nothing of its owner?

The year was 1960 and America was still in the throes of its long-term love affair with motorized transportation. Tail fins, chrome grillworks, decorative portals, and distinctive taillights defined each car as a potential classic. And every other guy was a shade-tree mechanic with grease under his fingernails and a steady confidence in his heart that he could fix just about anything.

We'd moved to the edge of town, miles from the nearest sidewalk and blocks from the nearest paved road.

It was in this rural setting that my next motorized mode of transportation materialized.

Dad bought the ancient little tractor to level the yards around the housing development he was building near Baseline Lake. It was a small temperamental beast with enough levers, knobs, and gears to operate a spaceship to the moon. It was wonderful! It was also old enough to be missing most of the nonessential parts.

Once Dad got the tractor running, he proceeded to teach me the finer points of putting it through its paces. "To raise and lower the front blade," he said, "you have to pull the lever toward you to release the lock that holds it in place." His massive arm slipped the lever over, and he lowered the blade. "Now you try it."

I pulled. I tugged. I wedged my back against the seat and my feet against the floor plate and managed to raise the blade about an inch. Dad thought for a moment and remarked, "We'll have to grease the gears to that, won't we?" It turned out that the three-pronged plow on the back of the tractor worked pretty much the same way, although I could actually get it to go up and down.

"Now, the really tricky part of driving this tractor," he pointed out, "is mastering the clutch. You've watched me work the clutch on the pickup. I ease up on the gas, push in the clutch, and shift gears. Then working the gas pedal and clutch pedal at the same time, you have to slowly let out the clutch as you give it some gas—it's all in the feel."

I'd watched Dad change gears thousands of times and knew the sequence by heart. However, there's a big difference between knowing something in your head and knowing it in your feet. Like most things in life, you have to develop a "feel" before you can successfully do it.

"The little tractor works the same way, except you have to push the clutch pedal in twice instead of just once," Dad said. "The pickup is new and has synchronized gears. The tractor is pretty old, and it has what's called a double clutch. You push it in once to take it out of gear and then you push it in again to put it in the next gear. Watch me." Dad got on the tractor, fired it up, and began the steps he'd just outlined. The clutch went in, and Dad slipped the tractor out of gear. But that was as far as he got. The clutch pedal just sat there on the floor.

"Hmm?" he said. "Seems the spring that's supposed to pull the clutch pedal back up is missing!" He reached down and pulled the clutch pedal up with his hand while he pushed the gas pedal with his foot. The little tractor chugged ahead.

While Dad called around to see about fixing the problem, I sat atop the tractor, turning the steering wheel, and working the front blade and back plow. When he came back, he said, "It's gonna be a couple of weeks before we can get a return spring for the clutch installed. If you were a monkey, you could push and pull the clutch pedal with your foot." I took off my left shoe, wrapped my toes around the pedal, and pulled it up.

For the next couple of hours, we practiced the fine art of "barefoot double clutching." I killed the tractor hundreds of times without moving it an inch. Then I graduated to the jerk and die; that's when the tractor would lunge ahead a couple of feet before expiring. During those two hours, I ran the gamut of emotions. When I was close to tears and frustrated beyond words, Dad believed for both of us. Through it all, he was a constant stream of encouragement and suggestions.

Finally, with the engine racing near the red line, I successfully got the little beast to motor forward. Unfortunately, my attempt to get it into the next gear resulted in another mechanical death. But now I knew what it *felt* like. Encouraged, I tried again. That one small success led to another, and before long I was batting close to .500 in the double-clutch department.

It would take a few more days before I could start from a dead stop on a hill, but on level ground, I was near perfection. Then came the day when I was ready to try my hand at leveling the ground in the backyard of one of Dad's houses. That was also the day I discovered that driving involves much more than the mere mastery of the mechanics. The world of driving isn't a level playing field where you are the only object in play.

Everything was going so well. I'd managed to scrape a couple of shovelfuls of dirt loose with the back plow and spread it out with the front blade. Under Dad's watchful eye, his son—the child prodigy—was coming into his own. He parked his pickup at the bottom of a short incline in the backyard and went to check on his building crew. I continued to level the ground above the incline, and my confidence grew with each pass. Then I decided to move on to the incline itself.

The scientific community is still at a loss when it comes to understanding all that's involved in the Law of Gravity. The planets attract in known and unknown ways. Centripetal and centrifugal forces figure into the mysterious grand scheme of things. And the theories surrounding the interplay of subatomic particles are still being refined. But there is one thing everyone knows for sure—gravity always wins.

I was double clutching barefoot with the best of them when the little tractor started to crab sideways down the incline. Dad hadn't covered that in his instructions. I tried speeding up. I tried slowing down. I tried pointing the tractor up the slope. Nothing worked. Like a moth to a flame, the little tractor continued its slide down the slope directly toward Dad's pickup truck.

I've heard it said that the adrenaline rush during a crisis allows you to take in every speeding detail as if it were happening in slow motion. In this case, the tractor and I *were* in slow motion. I had plenty of time to experience every terrifying moment . . . the sound of the front blade creasing the side of the pickup, starting in the middle of the door and working its way to the back wheel well . . . the tractor's tires rubbing on the rim of the front wheel well. It seemed to take forever. The damage done, I finally gave up and turned off the tractor.

All my enthusiasm for driving was replaced by a sickening dread in the pit of my stomach. My heart pounded in my ears, and it felt as if someone had poured a load of quick-dry concrete over my entire body. *This is way worse than breaking a window with an ill-aimed rock*, I thought. *My allowance for the next ten years won't pay for the damage.* There wasn't one thing I could do to make it better. All that was left was the long trek into the house to tell Dad about my handiwork.

He came out and surveyed the damage without a word. Then he put his arm around my shoulder, gave me a hug, and together we pulled the little tractor away from the pickup truck.

Once he'd moved his truck well away from the battlefield, he said, "You know, part of driving is figuring out where the trouble spots are before you get there, and a whole lot of driving well comes from plain old experience. I'd say you've made remarkable progress this afternoon. Think you can finish

YOU DON'T NEED A LICENSE FOR EVERYTHING

Alvin Straight is a seventy-three-year-old cowboy with heart trouble. He doesn't have a driver's license, but then he doesn't have a car. What he does have is a 1966 John Deere riding lawn mower and a desire to reconcile with his estranged younger brother, Lyle, before he dies. The problem is, Lyle lives about three hundred miles away.

If you saw the movie *The Straight Story*, you know what happens. Alvin drives to Mt. Zion on his riding lawn mower. It takes him about six weeks to get there, and along the way, we discover that a five-mile-an-hour pace can be just about right.

I like Alvin. His little tractor got away from him too. You just can't foresee everything that might happen, but he doesn't beat himself up over it, and no one else does either. They just help him out with his problem and get him on the road again. Sounds pretty true to life, if you ask this old double-clutch tractor man. In fact, it is a true story.[29]

leveling the yard?" Just like that, my Dad set me free and wiped my driving record clean.

I've driven just about every kind of motorized transport you can name. From dump trucks to small airplanes, from a motorcycle with suicide clutch to a 1958 Volkswagen bus that had been rolled twice (not by me) and had to be double clutched through the first two gears. I've also learned to look ahead for trouble spots and been spared countless problems in traffic and in life. Of course, one of life's most enjoyable (and entertaining) activities has been passing along Dad's admonition to novice drivers, "You have to slowly let out on the clutch as you give it some gas—it's all in the feel."

WHAT MY DAD TAUGHT ME

When mistakes happen, as they inevitably do, think of them as opportunities to bestow mercy.

> *Freedom is not worth having if it does not*
> *include the freedom to make mistakes.*
> —*Mahatma Gandhi*

HOW YOU SEE
WHAT YOU SEE
MAKES ALL
THE DIFFERENCE

SECTION IV

DiRECTiON FiNDERS

You can't live in Boulder, Colorado, for long without being drawn to the mountains. They are a constant presence that orients the most disoriented of us on the Piedmont Plateau. "The mountains are to the west," Dad would say. "Find the mountains, and you will always know which direction you're headed." He rehearsed that truth almost as often as he pointed out how to find the North Star.

"Locate the Big Dipper; use the two stars opposite the handle to draw an imaginary line, and look for a bright star along that line five times as far away as the distance between those two stars. (It helps if you look in the direction of the opening to the Big Dipper rather than in the direction of its bottom.)"

I can hardly go outside on a clear night without working out the location of the North Star and rehearsing my father's words to anyone who happens to be nearby. But some direction finders reside beneath the surface, orienting your life beyond the realm of the compass—if you can see them.

LiTTLE RED

Palestine, Texas, was home to the best climbing tree I ever conquered, and my dad's favorite aunt, Aunt Gertrude. Aunt Gertrude was known to most folks as "Little Red." She was not quite five feet tall, and once a redhead, always a redhead (even if you eventually have to get it out of a bottle).

Mom and Dad let me spend a week at a time with Great Aunt Gertrude. Little Red was widowed young but never grew old. She was my own personal Peter Pan. She taught art and the art of living in her home to hundreds of students. Little Red kept track of her former students and their spouses and children decades down the road. She traveled to Europe to see the great works of art, could discuss any subject you cared to introduce with informed insight, and owned an old car with a rumble seat.

When I was five, she made me spaghetti with one meatball for breakfast, lunch, and dinner. She also prayed for me every day of my life. No wonder she was Dad's favorite aunt. I can also see why Dad hauled me out to Palestine, Texas, and Aunt Gertrude's every chance he got; he was taking me back to the place and person who taught him to see life with an artist's eye.

Little Red could see around the edges—search beneath the surface. You have to find the proper point of view before you can understand the essence of a thing and capture it on canvas or with words. That was Little Red's charm—she took time to study the verities of life, committed them to canvas, and placed them in her students' hearts. She was patient enough to look until she saw.

Little Red lived in a cluttered little house in a sleepy little town that encouraged a sensible pace with plenty of rest stops. She took small steps. A child could keep up with her—and many did. Even when I grew well over six feet tall, I found that my long stride naturally shortened and slowed around Aunt Gertrude. She'd wrap her arm through mine, look up into my face, and give me a smile that seemed to say, "Who you travel with is more important than how fast you get there."

Over the years my visits with Little Red shrunk from days to hours. Life was fast and full. Who had time to reflect or listen? Still something drew me to her, and I kept pointing the car in her direction. For a few hours she would call me out of my fast-food world and into a parlor of aromatic teas, lingering conversations, and the

ALIVE TO BEAUTY

I wonder how many of us are truly alive to beauty. In *The Evidential Power of Beauty*, Thomas Dubay writes, "A moment's reflection makes it clear that there is in the human family a continuum from the keenly alive and responsive individual to the colorless, insensitive, and uninspired one."

The difference between being alive or dead to beauty seems to be a matter of connectedness or detachment. Those dead to beauty tend to be self-centered and vain; their self-trap renders them incapable of experiencing deep beauty. Those alive to beauty tend to have maturity that provides beauty a place to abide. They are rooted in the spiritual and thus connected to the Author of Beauty. They are able to love, and that opens the eyes of the heart to see deeply and truly. They have a thankful heart of praise able to celebrate and respond to the wonder of something beyond themselves and share it with others.[31]

I ran into Kurt Beerline right after writing this insert. He offered a simple acrostic for those who would develop an aliveness to beauty—S.T.O.P.—Slow down, Taste, Observe, and Ponder. (Little Red would have liked that.)

studied art of looking closely at life.

She set about to teach me the same things she'd taught my dad, like "God's not in a hurry"; "the mature must shorten their stride and slow their pace for the sake of the young as well as the immature"; "the horizon is often clearer in the company of those who have nearly reached the end of their road"; and "eating spaghetti three times a day is perfectly acceptable when you're five years old."

You had to slow down to appreciate the richness of Little Red's world. Learning to see around the edges and beneath the surface always eludes the hurried. Now that I'm able to catch my breath, I see that she was right; there's so much more to life than meets the eye.

Thanks, Dad, for taking me back to the Little Red you knew as a boy. I now see why you did.

WHAT MY DAD TAUGHT ME

You can improve your eyesight by spending time with those who have a better outlook on life.

*The things that slow you down seldom
end up being the things that hold you back.*

—Gary Stanley

MARY'S LAKE AND NEVER-SUMMER-LAND

One blustery day in late summer, Dad and I were exploring the topology around Estes Park, Colorado. The Twin Owls (a rock formation) looked down on us from their perch across the valley—they had become old friends of mine by the late summer of 1958.

Because Dad was a land developer with a dream of building a mountain frontier village, replete with a hotel and entertainment center near Estes Park, we spent many hours exploring the mountains. We hiked the surrounding meadows on the east side of town and climbed Ram Horn Rocks for a better view of the area and Mary's Lake.

A cold wind promised an early autumn, and Dad enfolded me in his overcoat. Bundled up, leaning back against his warm body, I looked out at the world through the opening of an unbuttoned slit between the folds of his coat. From our rocky perch, we observed the wind rippling and churning the surface of the lake. Miniature whitecaps were quickly spent and reborn. Across the way, a stand of aspen flickered green and gray as its silver dollar leaves flipped back and forth in the invisible breath that stirred the valley.

"What do you see?" Dad asked. It was his favorite question.

What did I see? I saw what any child would see—rocks and water and trees. I reported the same to Dad and then turned the question to him, "What do you see, Dad?"

He hugged me close and described the scene behind the scene. "Do you know why the rocks we're standing on are called the Ram Horn Rocks?" he asked quietly. "The mountain sheep climb up here at night to get away from the wolves. The bighorns can climb what the wolves can't. Up here they can sleep without fear. We're literally standing on a piece of God's protection for His creatures. He's like that. God doesn't leave us to fend for ourselves. He cares for us.

"When I look at Mary's Lake, I can almost make out a giant footprint. I wonder if God strolled through here as He fashioned this valley. He is so intimately acquainted with His creation. He shaped this place knowing that one day you and I would stand here enjoying His work. And you know what? He hoped it would remind us of Him.

"Those trees on the side of the mountain are aspen. Remember how I showed you their scarred trunks where the deer had eaten away the bark when there was nothing else for them to eat? They never eat the bark all the way around the trunk because that would kill the tree. Somehow God planted that information inside them. A month from now, the leaves will have turned, and we'll find a mountain of gold winking at us. I think the sight of that mountain will bring a bigger smile to God's face than all the gold man can dig out of the ground."

● ● ●

On another day Mom, Dad, and I drove to the top of Trail Ridge (elevation: 12,000-plus feet)—Never-Summer-Land as the Indians called it. After a cup of hot chocolate at the lodge, we parked next to a permanent snow pack. Mom threw the first snowball and soon ducked back into the warmth of the car. Dad and I eventually set off across the snow.

On a bare patch of ground warmed by the sun, Dad got down on his knees and showed me a forest in miniature. His big hands pulled back the summer grass, and he pointed out a bouquet of flowers that would fit on the head of a pin.

"Up here life takes place on a small scale," he taught me. "There's little oxygen, and the growing season is measured in days rather than months. Only the hardy survive. It almost looks cruel, doesn't it? So much struggle for so little gain. But, oh, the beauty rewarded for all the effort!

A gnarled tree on the edge of the timberline has a glory all its own that the tall straight ponderosa farther down the mountain knows nothing about."

Dad loved the mountains. He found wonders everywhere, and they all seemed to point him back to his Creator. Live in Colorado for long, and it's easy to take the glory of the Rockies for granted. I don't think he ever did. The wonder never settled into the background for him. He was too familiar with how it all fit into God's grand narrative for that to ever happen.

Last year my wife and I moved back to the Boulder area and the mountains of my youth. I can't help but look for them whenever I'm outside . . . can't help but think of the Divine Majesty

THE SACRED ROMANCE

"**O**nce upon a time the Western world had a story. Imagine you lived in the High Middle Ages. Your world was permeated with Christian imagery. You marked the days by the sound of the church bells and the weeks and months according to the liturgical calendar. You lived in *anno domini,* the year of our Lord.... The architecture of the cathedral, the music, literature, and sculpture all gave you a vision of transcendence, reminding you of the central elements of that great story ... all of your personal experiences would be shaped and interpreted by that larger story.

"But you don't live in the Middle Ages.... It's not Pentecost, it's time for spring training ... and the biggest taste of transcendence is the opening of the ski season. ... The central belief of our time is that there is no story."

But there is a story, and it's true, and there's a part in it exclusively for you.[32]

who created them. And when I do, I remember my own place in God's infinite story.

You taught me well, Dad; the lesson stuck, along with the question, "What do you see?" More and more, I am seeing the way you did, Dad. I see God too.

WHAT MY DAD TAUGHT ME

It's not so hard to find your place in God's story when the Author's presence is so clear.

> *The real voyage of discovery consists not in seeing new landscapes, but in having new eyes.*
>
> —Marcel Proust

REAL INDIANS DON'T WEAR UNDERWEAR

I am a typical American—a blend of English, Irish, Scot, German, Cherokee, and who knows what else. I can track my ancestral roots all the way back to a prime minister in England during the American Revolution. I can also track them back to an enterprising thief who stole the county seat and moved it to Wheeler, Texas. I have relatives who have ridden with the Texas Rangers, and I have relatives who have been chased by Texas Rangers.

What has all this to do with underwear you ask? I'll tell you. Everything! Dress and culture go hand in glove, or foot in moccasin. Fashion tastes are forever tied to culture and upbringing. You don't wear an overcoat in the jungle; you don't wear sandals in the Arctic. And if you want to dress the part of a buckskin-wearing, arrow-shooting

Indian, you don't wear underwear under your leather apron—totally destroys the effect, like one of those "B" movies where the Indians ride horses with blankets thrown over saddles.

These were my three- and four-year-old arguments with Mom. She wasn't convinced. "I don't want you 'shooting the moon' for the neighbors," she scolded. "What if you were hit by a car and taken to the hospital and you didn't have any underwear on?" Whoever heard of an Indian being hit by a car?

Fortunately, Dad understood the importance of authenticity, and he was able to win Mom over to "our" way of thinking. So, in the privacy of our backyard, I got to be a real Indian sans underwear. There's still a photo or two of me halfway up a leaning tree or dancing around my teepee, showing a daring bit of derriere while on the warpath. My Native American persona has been captured for all time. But there's more! I also had a theme song:

I'm a little Indian, ugh, that's me.
They call me Hiawatha, that's my name you see.
When I'm on the warpath, you can tell,
Oooooooh! Oooooooooh! That's my yell.
(There's more but I'll spare you.)

By the time I was five years old, I had graduated to a more socially acceptable, bare-chested, fringed-buckskin britches look, replete with rubber hunting knife and beaded belt. At the age of nine, I joined all of the other boys in the neighborhood and got a Mohawk haircut (just like the one James "Book 'em, Danno" MacArthur was sporting in the Disney movie, *The Light in the Forest*, 1958). I had this

Indian thing down. I milked that drop of Cherokee blood from my great-great-great-grandmother for all it was worth.

Within a week all but one of us had decided a burr haircut was a much cooler look than a Mohawk. It would be decades before the punk rock scene revived that particular hairstyle.

Funny, what's important to us at different seasons of life—what captures the imagination. Whether it's the conviction that a tattoo or pierced body part is essential to our emerging personalities, or the certitude that sporty cars will keep us young in our middle age, we all inhabit our dreams from time to time. It's important that we do.

Dad encouraged my role-playing and wasn't above a bit of pretending himself. We had

MAKING DREAMS COME TRUE

According to psychologist William James, "Ninety-five percent of us live on 5 percent of our potential." And Os Guinness notes, "God has created us and our gifts for a place of His choosing and we will only be ourselves when we are finally there." However, for many of us, our dreams remain just that—dreams. How can we ever live our dreams?

It is surprising how many of us are afraid to surface our deepest desires. John Eldredge concludes that we have three choices in life: "(1) to be alive and thirsty, (2) to be dead, or (3) to be addicted" (by lesser things that will never nourish our souls). "What do you want?" writes Eldredge. "Don't minimize it; don't try to make sure it sounds spiritual; don't worry about whether or not you can obtain it. Just stay with the question until you begin to get an answer. This is the way we keep current with our hearts."[33]

quite a collection of beards, hats, masks, rubber noses, and big feet. They never gathered dust. He loved to stir the imagination and thought if you dressed the part, you just might figure out why it was so appealing in the first place and decide whether to pursue it or not.

I've long dreamed of being a writer with a green cardigan, khakis, and loafers. But I've long accepted that with my receding hairline, the Mohawk is no longer an option—probably just as well.

WHAT MY DAD TAUGHT ME

Step wholeheartedly into your dreams. Some of them might just come true.

> *Clothes make the man. Naked people*
> *have little or no influence on society.*
>
> —*Mark Twain*

WHY THE DEER CROSSED THE ROAD

om, Dad, and I were packed in our green Rambler on one of our many trips to Palestine, Texas, to see Dad's favorite aunt, Little Red. We were traveling along a two-lane road that cut through an East Texas forest at dusk when Dad noticed a deer running alongside our car. The doe was so close to our car, I could almost reach out the window and touch her!

At first it seemed as though the deer was preparing to catch a ride (like a cowboy pacing a train on his horse before leaping aboard). We weren't going all that fast for a car, but the doe was moving flat out. I'd seen plenty of deer dart across the road or freeze in a car's headlights. I'd never seen one pace a car. The deer started to fatigue, head drooping and tongue hanging out, but still she ran.

When you find yourself in an unexpected contest, it's natural to jockey for position, lean into the steering wheel, and push the pedal to the floor. Dad did none of those things. Instead, he slowed down, worried that the deer would run herself into the ground. As he slowed, the deer gathered herself and jumped directly in front of us and crossed to the other side of the road.

Looking back on that odd little event, I think the deer simply wanted to get to the other side. But once committed, she found herself racing us to a point that wasn't stationary. We were blocking her goal—stretching the finish line. If Dad hadn't slowed down, I think the deer would have dropped.

I've been in a few road competitions myself. Hard not to go for the win, especially if the other guy just cut me off, slowed down in the fast lane, or decided to ride my bumper. Hard not to get caught up in the moment and start judging motives, jumping to conclusions, and exerting my rights. Some of my most insightful and impassioned lectures have been given from behind a steering wheel. I don't think they've been all that well received. Luci assures me they haven't.

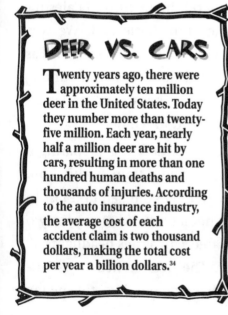

DEER VS. CARS

Twenty years ago, there were approximately ten million deer in the United States. Today they number more than twenty-five million. Each year, nearly half a million deer are hit by cars, resulting in more than one hundred human deaths and thousands of injuries. According to the auto insurance industry, the average cost of each accident claim is two thousand dollars, making the total cost per year a billion dollars.[34]

I remember the time a 240-Z pulled right in front of me from a side street. I nearly ran right up its bumper when it didn't pull away from me. Whoever heard of a car with that kind of muscle taking a turn like that and *not* speeding up? The only thing I could do was whip around the "Z" and cut back in—no time to stop. Prepared to give my "lecture" to some kid driver, I looked in the mirror and saw a little old granny scared plumb out of her rouge. I never figured a car like that would be driven by someone who wouldn't put it through its paces.

I can remember Dad saying right after he yielded the right of way to another driver, "It doesn't matter if you're dead right or dead wrong—you're still just as dead." I've been slow when it comes to believing the best about those I share the road with. But I have no excuse; I had a great teacher.

On a two-lane road, closed in by an East Texas forest, my dad modeled for me the very things he hoped I'd one day learn. He didn't toy or tease one who was winded and confused. My dad let the other guy win. He looked to see what course he might take for the sake of another.

WHAT MY DAD TAUGHT ME

Life isn't a competition.

> *Don't take the actions of others personally.*
> *Odds are they weren't thinking about you at all.*

TODDLE HOUSE AND THE NEWSPAPER BOY

Whatever happened to the Texas Toddle House? I expect it's gone the way of the New York automats, both innovative marvels of technology and design in their day. They could hardly have been more different.

The automat was the height of impersonal dining. Put a couple of quarters in the slot next to the small glass door and pull out an entrée, vegetable, or dessert. No need to wait in line, place an order, or wait for someone to cook up your meal. Strictly do-it-yourself. You could literally dine with a hundred other New Yorkers and never talk to a soul.

A Toddle House was an intimate counter grill—a twenty-four-hour, in-your-face, one-man show. Long before there was a Benihana chef, with his twirling knives and culinary artistry, there was the Toddle House cook. A good Toddle House man (or woman) could keep twelve counter customers in food, drink, and conversation and still have time to ring up your bill, wipe the counter, wash the dishes, and scrape the grill. No locks on the door—it was always open, whether you were an early riser or a late-night rider. Want to sit at a booth or a table in the corner instead of the counter? Find another joint.

The three things I liked best about Toddle Houses were chocolate cream pies, high counter stools that spun around, and Dad. Dad was a natural born conversationalist, and he was never more in his element than when he was in a Toddle's. There you could talk about anything. No subject was off limits, including politics, religion, or life in general. If you had an opinion, you were welcome to put your elbows on the counter and wade right in.

Dad liked his coffee weak—always ordered it "half hot water." And when it came time to pay his bill, he'd look it over, nod his head, and his smile would slide to the side of his face. "Not sure you got this right," he'd say. "Seems you charged me full price on the coffee. But I asked for it half hot water. Only seems fair you'd charge me half price on a thing like that."

Such an absurd thing to say! He caught more than one Toddle House proprietor off guard. But most gave as good as they took. Verbal swords drawn, the mock battle over the bill would begin. "There are additional fuel costs in getting that water hot," the cook would say. "Special service charges. And now I have to clean the hot-water pot!" A sacred ritual had been evoked.

The message and the words didn't match up, but the meaning was always clear, *We're both wonderful absurdities of God's best work, meant to be enjoyed. Have a great day!* Dad walked in a stranger and left a friend. Names were given and remembered, and Dad seldom had to remind a Toddle House cook that he liked his coffee "half hot water."

Of course that wasn't the only ritual I observed from my perch atop a green counter stool next to my dad. We visited the same Toddle House off and on long enough to know the regulars. An unkempt newspaper boy ended his daily paper route at the same Toddle House each morning. He always ordered a cup of coffee and a donut. He ate his meal in silence, and the Toddle House man always charged him fifteen cents—no tip. This bothered me. Boys weren't supposed to drink coffee, and I knew a cup of coffee and a donut were at least a quarter. So why did the newspaper boy get a discount over the rest of us? It wasn't fair!

One day after the boy had left, I asked Dad what was going on. Dad looked at me, and then he seemed to look at something you couldn't see with the physical eye. "Gary," he said, "that boy gets up and puts in several hours before he goes to school. He has to work. So most of what he makes delivering papers goes for groceries. I'm sure the fellow behind the counter would gladly give him coffee and a donut for nothing. But the boy's not looking for a handout. It would make him feel less than a regular customer. So he pays what he can afford. His meal costs him far more than ours when you look at it that way."

I think that was the first time I ever considered that there might be more than one way to look at something—that there might be more to life than meets the eye. I never thought to ask how Dad knew that boy's history. Maybe he cared enough to ask. Maybe he just got close enough to see what often passes unnoticed.

I'm not sure why that particular story has stuck with me all these years. I suspect I wasn't more than four or five when it happened. But now, forty-five years later, I can still see the unkempt newspaper boy hunched over his cup of coffee.

I wonder what ever happened to him? Did he mature into a man able to balance his need for independence with the knowledge that we all need some help along the way? Jesus said that what we do for the least of us, we do for Him. Maybe Jesus resided in that boy, and the Toddle

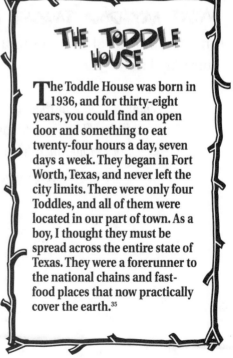

THE TODDLE HOUSE

The Toddle House was born in 1936, and for thirty-eight years, you could find an open door and something to eat twenty-four hours a day, seven days a week. They began in Fort Worth, Texas, and never left the city limits. There were only four Toddles, and all of them were located in our part of town. As a boy, I thought they must be spread across the entire state of Texas. They were a forerunner to the national chains and fast-food places that now practically cover the earth.[35]

man will discover to his surprise that his reward in Heaven far exceeds the extra dime he daily slipped into the register after the boy left.

Me? I still struggle with an overly acute sense of justice. I want things to meet my standard of fairness, but the fact is, God created a world that doesn't allow me to do so. Life isn't fair on this side of eternity, but it is good—whether you're the one who gets a discount or the one who doesn't need a discount. That's been a hard lesson for me to learn—not an easy thing to balance. It takes a careful eye to discern the difference. I first learned that in a Toddle House because my dad explained it to me.

WHAT MY DAD TAUGHT ME

There's almost always more to the story than you currently know.

> *When we come to the end of life, the question*
> *will be, "How much have you given?"*
> *not "How much have you gotten?"*
>
> —George Sweeting

THE GRAVEYARD ROMANTIC

A simple brass plaque on my dad's grave reads, "G. L. Stanley 1914-1962." The only ornamentation is two sprigs of evergreen in the corners. In the first year after he died, a lawn-mower blade scored the surface with three deep gouges. They've since worn away. Dad's grave is thirty-seven paces south of the bell tower and fifteen paces west—just off the flagstone path and just off the Longmont Diagonal. There are two plots next to it—one for Mom and one for me.

The tall row of poplars that lined the southern border of the cemetery is gone. The empty field to the north is now filled with Calvary Bible Church and its parking lot. But little else has changed in the graveyard itself over the past three decades. What has changed is me.

Over the years I've often stood by that grave and tried to talk out the confusions in my life. I wondered what

Dad would think about my latest venture, failure, or success. It was a practiced discipline of acknowledging that he was long gone and that an empty shell was all that lay beneath the surface.

I remember taking a girl or two out there—suppose I hoped to elicit sympathy or demonstrate the depth of my soul to an impressionable young thing. They weren't all that impressed. Usually, I felt like a fool walking back to the car after my heartfelt performances so full of myself. I was the tragic, conflicted hero plumbing the depths of soulish angst . . . Romeo in search of his Juliet . . . the brooding Heathcliff wandering the English Moors. I was a mess, and any sensible girl saw right through me. They were all sensible.

One winter's day, after a few inches of new snow, I was back at Dad's grave. I'd been away at graduate school. It had been a long time. I seldom had to share the cemetery with anyone else unless I brought them along. Today was different.

A bent little figure, huddled against the cold, was wandering around another part of the cemetery. The white-haired woman seemed confused. Her random tracks through the snow spoke of her search for some misplaced thing—a loved one.

"Can I help you?" I asked.

The round, wrinkled face looked up at me as I approached. "I buried my husband last week," she answered, "and I can't find his grave. The snow has covered everything, and I can't remember where they've put him."

I know what it's like to feel disconnected—adrift. As I looked into her face, she seemed familiar. Her snow-white hair framed her sad eyes and face. I knew that face.

"Mrs. Alpers?"

My query startled her. She searched my face for a moment and said, "Yes, I'm Mrs. Alpers."

"You were my fifth-grade teacher at Martin Park. I'm Gary Stanley."

"I remember . . . your mother was also a teacher, wasn't she?"

"Yes, that's right."

And so began our friendship. I took her to the office, and we found her husband's plot number and soon matched it to the newly dug grave.

I felt a bit more like my dad that day in the cemetery—less

WHY GO ON?

Why is it that sometimes when one spouse in a long-term marriage dies, the other spouse dies soon after but from no apparent physical cause? These incidents are called the "phenomena of sudden death." This sudden death phenomena happens in the animal kingdom as well—not to those who have lost a mate, but to those who are cornered or scared.

C. P. Richter wanted to know the cause of this sudden death phenomenon, so he selected as his subjects some of the most tenacious survivors on the planet—sewer rats. He placed one rat in a vat of water and timed how long it took the rat to drown. After hundreds of trials, he concluded that the average sewer rat could swim for several minutes—even hours—before finally drowning. Then Richter changed one aspect of his experiment.

After leaving the rat in the vat of water long enough for it to reach apparent fatigue, Richter would rescue the rat. After a short time he then put it back in the water and started his stop watch again. He repeated this exercise hundreds of times. It turns out that a sewer rat that has been rescued once doesn't swim for several minutes or hours—it swims for days. The second group of rats averaged better than sixty hours of treading water before drowning. That's two and a half days!

Richter concluded that the first group of rats gave up in the face of a hopeless situation. In the second group, the rats had been rescued once, so the situation apparently didn't seem hopeless to them. With hope, each swam with all its heart, strength, and will.

The conclusion for humans is the same. We can't live without hope, and some spouses can't imagine life without their lifelong partners. However, there are no circumstances beyond hope; for we have a Rescuer who came once to save us, and we have His Word that He will come again.[36]

concerned about my own needs and more involved in meeting the needs of another, a rare event for one so often wrapped up in himself. Felt good. I didn't feel so alone either. I bet it was one of those secrets he would have shared with me if he'd lived. Perhaps he already had; it just took a long time for it to sink in.

Yes, I finally made an impression on a female during a graveyard visit. She wasn't the supple young thing of my dreams, but it did lead to romance. A few years later, I married my fifth-grade teacher . . . to her new eighty-year-old beau. Their children gave them away as I shouted the words of their vows, so they could hear spoken what their hearts already knew.

The octogenarians were only married three months when Mrs. Alpers (now Mrs. Leslie) became a widow for a second time. I lost track of her after that. Suspect she's resting next to her first husband. I think I'll check the next time I pay a visit to my dad's grave. . . .

She is.

WHAT MY DAD TAUGHT ME

A true romantic doesn't spend his time trying to get love; he's too busy giving it.

> *You're born. You suffer. You die.*
> *Fortunately, there's a loophole.*
>
> —*Billy Graham*

THE SMELL
OF A SHIRT

'**ve** been rummaging through all the stuff that belonged to my father. His suits, wing tips, and wide ties are long gone. So are his drafting table, business files, stamp collection, and one of Babe Ruth's autographed home-run balls he snagged as a boy during his brief stay in Detroit. Like old baseball cards and comic books, things that now seem priceless were deemed worthless and thrown out—clutter, space wasters, junk.

How often I have the urge to purge my life of stuff. Yet stuff is, well, the stuff of life. I still lug around Dad's old, green-marbled, sixteen-pound bowling ball. I've tried to use it, but the finger holes are too big for my hand. His fingers were thicker than mine. The leather bag has all but rotted away. What a foolish thing to hang on to! It just takes up space. What am I saving it for? I've no idea. It falls in the same category as many of the other items that fill a couple of cardboard boxes in my garage, items such as:

- A faded catalogue from the Stanley Furniture Store Dad sold before it amounted to much and two ornately carved high-back chairs from the Stanley Furniture Factory that I've been meaning to refinish

- A box of old magic tricks (Dad loved to perform his milk-pitcher trick, pretending to pour milk into someone's hat. The "secret" inner lining is too clouded for it to fool anyone today.)

- Some promotional materials from Ute Enterprises— a dream resort that died before its time

- Three worn-out Bibles

- An odd assortment of cuff links, tie clips, and penknives in an old jewelry box

- Dad's long-expired driver's license

- A vinyl 45-record with his voice on it urging me at the age of three to perform for Mammuddy (Grandmother) by counting to ten and singing "How Much Is That Doggie in the Window"—the first of many future performances

- A spotty collection of carpentry and mechanic's tools

- Dad's obituary notice and a stack of sympathy cards

- His grandfather's gold watch and a brass compass in which the blue-stained tip points South rather than North

- A plaque for "Stanley Hall" that was taken down after he was long forgotten

- Typed copies of James Thurber's stories he loved to tell (which I thought Dad wrote until I read Thurber for myself)

- Newspaper clippings and a couple of funny sermons

- A birth certificate that revealed Dad's real name was George Levi (For most of his life, he thought his name was just "G. L." It surprised Pop Pop and Mammuddy when they found his birth certificate years later; they'd forgotten what name they'd put on it!)

- Two blue-ribbon paintings by Little Red—one of a dog done entirely with straight lines and the other of a cat drawn only with curves

- His 30-06 rifle, 12-gauge shotgun, and a rusty 30-30

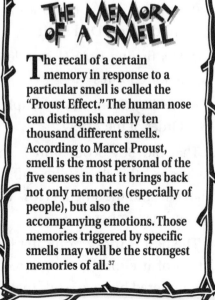

THE MEMORY OF A SMELL

The recall of a certain memory in response to a particular smell is called the "Proust Effect." The human nose can distinguish nearly ten thousand different smells. According to Marcel Proust, smell is the most personal of the five senses in that it brings back not only memories (especially of people), but also the accompanying emotions. Those memories triggered by specific smells may well be the strongest memories of all.[37]

which reportedly rode with the Texas Rangers and killed three men (It does have three notches on the stock.)

- A deerskin pelt that's too small to make anything out of
- His old hunting knife (It is the closest thing to what Tarzan must have carried that I've ever found.)
- A half dozen books of family histories, poetry, and inspiration
- Hundreds of photographs carefully sorted by Mom into five photo albums
- A stack of super-8 film (Of course, Dad was always the cameraman, so there's not much footage of him.)
- Two green canvas tents (We camped a lot.)
- A map and promotional materials for the last subdivision Dad built
- His fishing pole (I wonder if it will still cast?) and assorted lures
- His Boy Scout shirt, complete with Eagle Badge and Order of the Arrow

That old Boy Scout shirt is my favorite keepsake—the badges on the sleeve, the stiff, coarse canvas feel of the material, and the smell. I close my eyes, take a deep breath . . . and remember.

The past is tricky. You can't hang onto it, but you can't let go of it either. During a recent move, my wife and I encountered boxes of stuff that we seldom touch. I sorted through them to see if I could get rid of at least one box. I couldn't—bet you can't either.

Why do we keep things that only take up space? Precisely because they *do* take up space—in our hearts. If we threw the stuff away, we might not revisit the memories again, and the loss of memories is one of the most terrible losses of all. The past often sorts out the present when you finally figure out where to put it all.

WHAT MY DAD TAUGHT ME

You carry the memory of your dad with you from cradle to grave. How you carry it determines whether it is a burden or a blessing.

> *The past is a foreign country;*
> *they do things differently there.*

> —L. P. Harley

YOU DON'T HAVE TO SURVIVE IN ORDER TO SUCCEED

SECTION V

WHY PLAYING IT SAFE ISN'T SAFE

Disturb us, Lord, when we are too well-pleased with ourselves,

> when our dreams have come true because we dreamed too little,

> when we arrived safely because we sailed too close to the shore.

Disturb us, Lord, when with the abundance of the thing we possess,

> we have lost our thirst for the water of life;

> when having fallen in love with life,

> we have ceased to dream of eternity,

> and in our efforts to build the new earth,

> we have allowed our vision of heaven to dim.

Stir us, Lord, to dare more boldly, to venture on wilder seas,

> where storms will show Your mastery,

> where losing sight of land, we shall find the stars.

We ask You to push back the horizons of our hope,

> and to push us into the future in strength, hope, courage, and love.

—a prayer of Robert Darwell
(just prior to an operation in which he died)

ERROL FLYNN WANNABEES AND THE WOODEN POINTERS

I 've always suspected that the second life of a broken and worn-out pool cue was spent as a wooden pointer about three feet long—varnished but not stained—with a black rubber tip that never stayed put. It always had a chrome eyelet screwed into the bottom so you could kill hours trying to snag the hook sewn into the bottom of those windup window shades that hung on the tall windows at school.

It was a magical instrument—a big baton that meant business, not some wimpy conductor's wand that couldn't hurt a fly. We're talking hardwood here—stout, smooth, and powerful. The wooden pointer could turn the obscure into the center of attention. When the teacher aimed the wooden pointer at you, you could almost feel the cross hairs of a phantom rifle playing on your forehead.

One evening my childhood buddy, David, and I discovered ourselves in a basement classroom at church with two wooden pointers and no adult in sight! There must be a male gene especially created for such moments, an instinct for engagement that foregoes the niceties of reflection or possible ramifications.

"Swords" were crossed. We were Robin Hood and the Sheriff of Nottingham on the castle stairs, Zorro and Ricardo Montelban in the hacienda courtyard. *Parry. Thrust. Counter. Block. Leap. Run. Lunge. Spin. Whack. Swat. Knuckle rap. Yowwelll!* And then, just as we were getting the hang of it, swoosh! We were lifted off the ground in the grasp of a terrified adult supervisor who was certain we were nanoseconds away from "putting somebody's eye out."

Dad soon learned that his only son was a church hooligan with homicidal tendencies. He, however, took a different point of view. He knew a wooden pointer had a life beyond its intended use. He knew that a boy's imagination and zest ought to be celebrated, not squelched out of parental embarrassment. And he knew that a life filled with spontaneity and surprise is better than one stuffed with the mundane and predictable, even if the risks are higher. Dad lived that way himself.

• • •

Dad often said, "Better a man dissatisfied than a pig satisfied." In other words, better the chance of a full soul over the certitude of a full belly. Years before he had walked away from a secure job in corporate management to embrace the dream of being his own boss. It was a dream full of freedom and the risks that went with it. It was that decision that gave me access to a father who otherwise would have been locked behind an office door from nine to five.

It wasn't long after the wooden pointer incident that Mom and Dad took me to an open house at a day school for the arts—a magical place for young thespians to learn the crafts of the noblesse (those of royal rank). There were acting workshops, painting and dance classes, and fencing lessons!

It wasn't long before I'd donned a wire mask, padded vest, and oversized gloves and been handed a foil. My opponent was a regular at the school, a seasoned veteran in the gentleman's code of honor for such things. We took our marks, and when the signal was given, we commenced to have at it. He quickly deflected my weapon and boasted that he'd scored the first point when he touched the middle of my padded vest with the rubber point of his foil. Scored a point! What nonsense! What damage were you likely to induce aiming for the padded areas of your opponent?

I surveyed my opponent, almost completely covered to the thigh, and spied out the one vulnerable spot in this sport to my way of thinking. He continued to pursue his scoring system while I lowered my aim and scored a few points of my own. Nothing like the switchy side of a fencing foil to raise a whelp on the back of the legs of an opponent. I routed my opponent and chased him down the stairs with my best Indian war cry as I swatted away.

I never went back to that day school for the arts. And I never got the "be-careful-you-might-put-somebody's-eye-out" lecture from Dad. Perhaps he saw lurking deep within me the seeds of an overly cautious and fearful heart and had decided to let me play against the fear of unseen outcomes and risk.

THE WORLD WRESTLING FEDERATION HAS NOTHING ON ANCIENT ROME

Ancient wrestling matches weren't for the squeamish or timid. Hoping to see some clean takedowns, reversals, and figure-four leg locks? Better look elsewhere. During the time of the Roman Empire, little things like kicking, biting, and scratching were perfectly acceptable tactics in the world of wrestling. However, there was one way to be disqualified ... one hard and fast rule ... one boundary you just didn't cross in the fun and games of wrestling. You were never allowed to poke someone's eye out.[38]

I miss the carefree abandon of the little boy I once was. In later years a few failures and unanticipated consequences opened the door to my fearful heart. I became a worst-case scenario kind of guy who tried to control life's vagaries. Wooden pointers were replaced with predictable outcomes, and my soul was slowly starved.

Dad was right, "Better a man dissatisfied than a pig satisfied." It has taken me years to regain even a portion of the wonder that comes from opting for dreams over measured security. There are still those who would gladly offer a bowl of porridge for a birthright under the guise that some piggish security is better than the risk of ending up with nothing. Don't you believe it!

WHAT MY DAD TAUGHT ME

There are worse things than losing an eye—losing your soul is one of them.

> *Better to have failed at something you love,*
> *than to succeed at something you hate.*
>
> —*George Burns*

THE DAY i RAN AWAY AND HOW FAR i GOT

Ever run away from home? I did . . . only once. Once was enough.

I suppose there are lots of reasons to run away—hurt feelings, misunderstandings, a romanticized vision of life on the road, the hope that we will be missed, that constrained feeling that comes with boundaries and too many restrictions.

Running away looks a lot different today than it did in the 1950s. In a recent article on orphans, foster care, and the decay of the traditional family, it was no surprise that teenage runaways now number in the millions.[39] Many runaways would more accurately be called throwaways. They aren't running away from home; they never had one.

Picture today's runaway, and you probably envision life on the street, innocence lost, victimization, and a bad end. But life on the road wasn't always portrayed that way. There was a time when it was portrayed as a romantic adventure.

Remember the "Littlest Hobo?" Didn't think so. London, the Wonder Dog, had the lead in this black and white television series. I watched it after school most days. London lived the life of the road, meeting new friends, helping folks in crisis, and moving on with no thought of reward.

Now that I think of it, that was pretty much the story line of most of the old black and white westerns that dominated Saturday morning television. I suspect that was the dominant message of the day—leave home and make a difference. Anyway, "The Littlest Hobo" had a theme song that summed up what I'm trying to get at—still remember most of the words:

Travelin' around from town to town,
sometimes I think I'll settle down.
Can't help but wonder what's in store,
could be I've been here once before.
But I know I'd hunger to be free.
Roamin's the only life for me.
I'm driftin' the world is my friend.
I'm travelin' along the road without end.
(Roll credits.)

We were living in a small frame house in Fort Worth, Texas. The summer heat had sucked the life out of the neighborhood lawns. Brown was the dominant color. Asphalt streets cooked and sent vapors skyward, distorting the scene like a bad piece of glass. I felt confined, restricted; I needed to get away.

My folks probably had seen it coming. I wasn't reluctant when it came to voicing my opinions at home. They nodded, frowned, weighed my words. They probably remembered their own youthful dreams and perhaps Helen Keller's words that "Life is an adventure or it's nothing."

It was time for me to find my own way—strike out on my own, leave the nest, seek my fortune, embrace the life of the road. Dad gave me a manly pat and said he understood. Mom offered to pack me a lunch (even wrapped it up in a colorful handkerchief and tied in on the end of a stick so I could carry it over my shoulder). I didn't figure I'd need much, just the clothes on my back and my life savings (a bit under five dollars). "The road" would meet my needs and welcome me in.

Dad said, "Be sure to write." Mom said, "Come back for a visit whenever you can." They said, "We'll miss you."

I gave them my most mature wave of farewell, adjusted my load, and turned left at the end of the driveway. I glanced back to see them standing at the front door with their arms wrapped around each other, trying hard to be brave. I took a deep breath and held my head high, savoring my new independence. I was marching to the beat of a different drummer.

That's when I noticed a vague uneasiness in the pit of my stomach. Not one soul was visible as I hiked down the sidewalk. The neighborhood was empty. Alone in the world, I trudged on. No birds sang in cadence with my step. No

RiDiNG iNTO THE SUNSET

Hopalong Cassidy (the first good guy to wear a black hat) helped pioneer the popularity of the TV western. "Hoppy" became such an important role model for his young viewers that "good behavior" spots were eventually added to the end of each episode.

My dad once met the Cisco Kid on a plane and brought me an autographed photo of Cisco and his horse, Diablo. All 156 episodes of The Cisco Kid were made in color, though we all watched on black and white sets.

By 1960 the TV western dominated primetime seven nights a week. By my count, there were thirty-two western-type series broadcast during those years.[40]

catchy theme song came to mind. No rainbow broke the clear sky to calm my growing fears.

Why do the credits always roll as the cowboy hero rides out of town rather than into it? What did Hopalong Cassidy do between adventures? Where did Kit Carson sleep after the frontier family bid him farewell? What did the Cisco Kid eat after he polished off the picnic lunch the pretty town girl packed for him?

Coming to a crossroads in my life— a corner—I thought I'd rest for awhile. Sidewalk corners aren't really designed for sitting. With chin on my knees, feet in the dry gutter, heart a bit further down, the other side of the street didn't look as appealing as it had earlier in the day. I looked up and down the road as far as I could see—nothing. I checked my options and reviewed my prospects. They didn't look all that promising. That's when I came to my senses, realized my limitations, and found a reason to go home. *I'm not allowed to cross the street on my own. I'm only four years old!*

Running away from home could take me around the block, but it couldn't get me out of the neighborhood. The weight in my stomach lifted. I decided to eat the lunch Mom packed for me. *I should have brought along something to drink. Hmm, there's a half-finished bottle of pop in the frig. Wouldn't want it go stale. Some restrictions are a good thing.*

"I'm back!" I announced.

"Good to have you home, son," Dad said. "Remember running off a couple of times myself." Dad hugged me and told me of his own boyish attempts at independence and about repairing an old Model-T for a road trip to Detroit with his buddy, then coming back home. I'm quite sure he never let me out of his sight during my adventure with independence.

I was still a four-year-old. I knew little of life. There would be other times when I would set out on the path of independence with mixed success, still confusing the romantic ideal with the concrete reality. But there has always been a very present Father who never lets me out of His sight.

WHAT MY DAD TAUGHT ME

Independence comes in stages—it isn't wise to skip any of them along the way.

> *Home is the place where when you*
> *go there, they have to let you in.*
>
> —*Robert Frost*

iF YOU CAN'T FALL, YOU'LL NEVER LEARN

The gently sloping gravel road where I learned to ride a two-wheeler is now paved. The "road rash" on my knees healed up nicely decades ago, and the training wheels of my first bike are long gone, along with the bike. What remains are the memories of how it all began.

I started out with training wheels on my bike. Practicing in the confines of our concrete driveway, I seldom ventured out on the gravel road in front of the house. However, once I was proficient with the extra wheels, I began to think that the driveway was a poor substitute for the open road.

Ever try to ride a bike in gravel—even with training wheels? Pedaling through deep gravel is a bit like walking on marbles—a lot of movement in the wrong direction, usually down. The gravel monster suddenly seizes the front tire, and the handlebars are wrenched out of your grasp. The bike buckles in the middle, and you swan dive partway over the handlebars as you rearrange a couple of yards of gravel and some of the skin on your face. Kids didn't wear kneepads or helmets in the 1950s.

I still remember the day Dad removed the training wheels from my bike. Once we were down to two wheels, he had to steady the bike for me to mount, and then he ran alongside to compensate for my lack of balance.

Who'd ever believe that it is easier to balance something in motion than something at rest? I figured if you couldn't balance a perfectly still bike, there's little reason to think you'd have better success on one flying down the street.

"It's just one of those things you have to take on faith until you experience it for yourself," Dad said. "A moving bike is easier to balance than one standing still." It was kind of like trying to convince a baby bird that once out of the nest it would do what it had never done—fly. That kind of thinking needs a push to get started!

"Don't let go! I'm not ready!" I instructed.

THE PRICE OF SUCCESS

Walter Payton made his living carrying a football. Over his thirteen-year career he gained 16,726 yards on 3,838 attempts, making him the all-time leading rusher in the NFL. All told, Payton ran nearly nine miles on the football field after being knocked down or run out of bounds every 4.4 yards. Oh yes, he also scored 110 rushing touchdowns along the way.[41]

We slowly picked up speed as we reached the end of the driveway and turned onto the thinly graveled road. Dad trotted at my side, holding the back of the bike. "You're doing great, Gary. Keep your head up. Don't look at your feet. That's it." The voice in my ear began to sound a bit more distant. He'd let go! I was on my own. And he was right! It is easier to balance a moving bike than one standing still. Afraid to turn around to see where he was, I continued my wobbly descent down the gentle hill and coasted to a stop on the incline up the other side.

I'd done it! No more training wheels!

Dad taught me to ride a bike the same way his dad taught him, and a thousand other dads taught their sons. He held me up until he figured I could do it without him, and then he let go so I could see that it was true.

Luci and I recently got a couple of Schwinn "street cruisers" to ride around the neighborhood. I'm not interested in jumping curbs or seeing how fast I can go these days. Haven't fallen off a bike in a long time. But I do face other challenges in life, and the learning process is still pretty similar. I need someone to hold me up, give me a push, and then let go when the time is right.

WHAT MY DAD TAUGHT ME

There comes a point when you have to take off the training wheels and not worry so much about falling— or failing.

No one knows what he is able to do until he tries.

—*Publilius Syrus (50 B.C.)*

A REASON TO CRY

When I was nine, I witnessed my first staged temper tantrum. I suppose I'd seen them before, but this one caught my eye. Some little kid threw himself down on the floor and screamed his lungs out. This was not the sort of thing you could miss, even as a distractible nine-year-old. But what held my attention more was the response of the kid's dad—he gave in to his son's demand, and the crybaby walked out of the five-and-dime with his heart's desire of the moment. (I think it was a pack of LifeSavers.)

Well, what have we here? A magic formula for anything your heart desires? Definitely worth further investigation. After careful reflection and another week's observation in the ways of emotional blackmail and parental embarrassment, I was ready to make my move.

Please understand that my parents were not miserly toward their only son. I'm quite sure the rest of my relatives thought Mom and Dad shamelessly spoiled me, and they were probably right. However, for whatever reason, I had never felt the need to test their patience or public discomfort with a display of childish angst—until now.

The Woolworth five-and-ten-cent store was full of wonderful things like balsa airplanes, Pez dispensers, candy, and Slinkies. I have no idea what particular toy or candy I hoped to extort from my dad when I threw myself on the floor and howled. Nine is a bit old for that sort of thing, but I have always been a late bloomer, and you have to start sometime.

Dad observed my performance with little outward emotion. Then he bent down, picked me up, and said, "You know, son, the ability to get in touch with your emotions is a great gift. And I would never want you to think that it is inappropriate to cry in private or public. Tears can wash away a lot of pain, and God uses tears to reattach our heads to our hearts." (Okay, he didn't say that last bit. But it was the sort of thing he was capable of saying.) "Gary, I love you too much to ever want to take away your ability to cry, but I also love you enough to make sure that when you cry you have a good reason to cry."

His little speech caught me off guard. He was supposed to be embarrassed that his son was wailing and rolling around on the floor and then give in to my demands. Instead, he calmly talked to me about the nature of life. It was like he'd been waiting for the right moment to deliver this piece of sage advice he'd worked out in advance.

I immediately halted my performance to reflect on Dad's words. Unfortunately, I missed every one of the subtle points he was making. A few days later I gave my second and, as it turned out, last performance as a crybaby. No sooner had I launched into a mournful wail when Dad picked me up off the floor and repeated the bit about "giving me a good reason to cry." Guess you could say my career as a thrower of tantrums was cut short for health reasons.

I've only been spanked a handful of times in my life, and each one followed the same format. Dad would hold me close and calmly explain what I had done wrong and why some physical discipline would now be necessary. I was given the opportunity to recant my transgressions, and

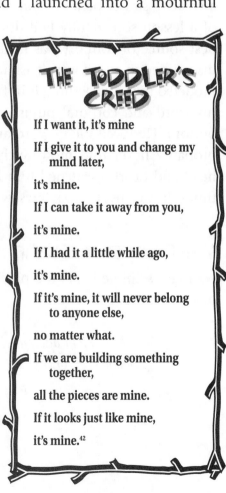

THE TODDLER'S CREED

If I want it, it's mine

If I give it to you and change my mind later,

it's mine.

If I can take it away from you,

it's mine.

If I had it a little while ago,

it's mine.

If it's mine, it will never belong to anyone else,

no matter what.

If we are building something together,

all the pieces are mine.

If it looks just like mine,

it's mine.[42]

Dad was as good as his word. He'd swat my bottom, and I was given a good reason to cry, which I did with all my heart.

One of the great lessons I learned from my half-dozen spankings was that the depth of my sincere repentance never affected the promised outcome. Dad's consistency was a sacred trust with him. I was not a repeat offender—a creative sinner perhaps, but not one to miss the point of a lesson so carefully laid down. I also knew that the best source of comfort was in the arms of the one who disciplined me. Dad wasn't ashamed to cry either, and he modeled that wonderful gift in front of me when he kept his word and corporal punishment was applied to my bottom. He loved me in word and deed. And though he probably never told me directly that tears connect the head and heart, I watched him live out that truth many times. It was just the way he saw it.

WHAT MY DAD TAUGHT ME

Loving discipline bears the pain of the offense with the one in need of correction.

A problem adequately stated is a
problem well on its way to being solved.

—R. Buckminster Fuller

THE THiRD WOLF CRY

Remember the kid who cried "wolf" one too many times? After awhile nobody believed him, and when he really needed help, no one responded to his cry. My dad loved to tell me that story. I was about to experience the truth of it firsthand.

My first wolf cry was my tantrum in the five-and-dime. My second cry of wolf happened a week later after which I decided "for health reasons" to give up the notion of becoming a crybaby. I had one more "wolf" in me that month, only this one was for real. I used it on a mountainside.

Mountains were made to climb, be they small or tall. To stand on top of them is one of life's clearest callings. Not that it's all that easy. Even if you do manage to get near the top, the "top" has a way of alluding you. Just when you think you've reached the highest point, you look around and discover yet a higher bit of rock a ways off—sometimes a long way off.

I'm not sure why Dad and I decided to have a go at this particular mountain. There was a pullout by the side of the road on the way to Estes Park and a nice steep slope just begging to be conquered. Mom decided to wait in the car and cheer us on.

We encountered plenty of shale at the beginning of the climb. Loose shale stirs up the dust, cuts the fingers, and makes a general nuisance of itself when you're trying to climb. The shale soon gave way to scrub brush and wild grass, but the slope was still pretty challenging. A hundred feet above the road, Dad reviewed a few of his patented mountain climbing rules: "Watch where you put your hands; there are snakes up here. Keep your feet pointed downhill, and if you ever start to slide, spread-eagle your arms and legs, don't roll; you'll just lose control if you do. Better a few scrapes and rock burns than a major tumble and some broken bones."

For some reason, a barbed-wire fence ran across the steepest part of the slope. I don't know what they hoped to keep fenced in (or out) or even how they managed to construct a fence there in the first place. Anything that could make it to the fence wouldn't have had any trouble getting over or under it—we didn't. At least we didn't on the way to the top. The trip back down was another matter.

It is usually easier to go up than it is to come down. Cats in trees know this, and I was about to learn it for myself. Dad was right behind me on the descent when I tried to step between the strands of barbed wire. Just as I stepped through, I began to slip on a patch of loose shale. Trying hard to catch myself, I grabbed the only thing within reach—the fence.

When I grabbed the fence, the fence grabbed me. I let go and wailed all the way to the bottom. Dad wasn't far behind, and once he saw my bloody hand, he pronounced it a "deep scratch" and told me to lower the vocal volume a bit. I scaled back my audible complaints to a serious whimper. Dad was not pleased. His son was still stuck in the crybaby stage, he reasoned. Mom wrapped my hurt paw in one of Dad's handkerchiefs, and we drove on to Estes Park.

We stopped at a clinic in the small mountain town to have my hand properly bandaged. The attendant took a good look at the wound and said I needed to have it stitched up. We'd have to drive back to Boulder for that. Dad began to think I might have had a reason to cry after all.

In the basement of Community Hospital, I lay on a gurney as some doctor shot Novocain into my hand, sewed up the cut, and then wrapped my hand in a big, stiff, white bandage. I carried my white badge of honor in a sling, cradling it with my good hand. The pain was gone from everywhere but Dad's eyes. "I'm sorry, son. I didn't think you were seriously hurt when I told you not to cry. I was wrong. Please forgive me."

The next afternoon when I came home from school, I found an unexpected present by the door. Dad had bought me a pair of junior skis that could be tied to my shoes, complete with a set of poles. I wasn't quite sure why he bought those toy skis for me. He hadn't given into my childish howls at the five-and-dime, and yet real tears resulted in something nice I hadn't even asked for. I think he wanted me to know his regret was real; the skis were a visible reminder. But I had a better one—my scar.

A few weeks after the accident, Dad brought me a tube of cream to rub into the developing scar. "Rub this on your palm, and it will lessen the scarring," he said. Then he gently rubbed in the sweet-smelling ointment. He kept doctoring it over the next few days, stressing its importance. Rubbing that scar with ointment became a habit with me until the scar all but disappeared a few years later.

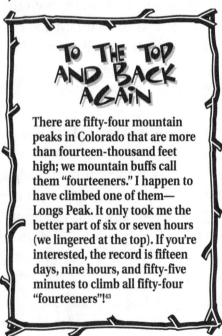

TO THE TOP AND BACK AGAIN

There are fifty-four mountain peaks in Colorado that are more than fourteen-thousand feet high; we mountain buffs call them "fourteeners." I happen to have climbed one of them— Longs Peak. It only took me the better part of six or seven hours (we lingered at the top). If you're interested, the record is fifteen days, nine hours, and fifty-five minutes to climb all fifty-four "fourteeners"![43]

I carry the reminder of that day on my left hand—a three-and-a-half-inch scar down the middle of my palm. It missed every major tendon, nerve, and muscle.

I carry several scars on my body from various surgeries, dog bites, motorcycle accidents, and the mountain-climbing incident with my dad. I heard some-where that you can store a lot of wisdom in your scars. I expect it's true. You certainly can store a lot of memories there, and the memory of the day my dad asked for my forgiveness couldn't be closer at hand.

WHAT MY DAD TAUGHT ME

Forgiveness and healing go hand in hand.

> *If you've overreacted or you're wrong, ask for forgiveness. That isn't going to lose your child's esteem. Not owning up to it will.*
>
> —Neil Anderson

YOU CAN'T RIDE A POLAROID

t was the smallest package under the tree that year. I don't remember what else I received (probably a toy I thought I couldn't live without, some clothes I didn't think I needed, and the pocketknife I still have stashed in a drawer although the point is broken off).

Every Christmas we drove from Boulder, Colorado, to Shamrock, Texas, over Raton Pass, across the high plains of the panhandle on the rolling two-lane called Highway 287, and finally along old Route 66. At the end of the long day was a multicolored Christmas tree just to the right of the front door, bearing hundreds of homemade and store-bought ornaments. The tree seemed to grow right out of the enormous pile of presents at its base.

Mammuddy, an odd blend of rouge, cologne, and the color purple, always rushed from the kitchen to kiss us. Pop Pop extended a bony hand that squeezed mine way too hard. And aunts, uncles, and first cousins I hadn't seen in a year sounded their greetings from all parts of the house.

The dominant world of plastics and computers was decades away, and most toys were still made of metal or wood. It was a time of Erector Sets, Lincoln Logs, and wind-up robots that sent sparks flying when scooted across the floor.

Every child in our family under the age of twelve (and a few older) surreptitiously searched the mound of presents during the evening in hopes of finding packages with their names on them. Wrapped mysteries were hefted, shaken, and pondered. *What might this gift hold? Underwear? A magic trick?* Too light to be a pack of playing cards, the smallest box with my name on it didn't fit any known gift category. Perhaps it was the control box to some mechanical marvel, or even money!

"Open this one last," Dad instructed.

Ah, so it is something special! Maybe a code book to a secret treasure hidden elsewhere! Christmas was a whole night away—eternity!

By midmorning every present of importance (those belonging to me) had been opened and the giver thanked ever so briefly. All that remained was "the gift," the tiny mystery forced to wait until every other present was unveiled. Finally! The prize! What I'd spend the rest of the day playing with! The one present I'd remember out of a lifetime of childhood presents!

Paper flew, tape broke, tissue shredded, and there it was . . . a black-and-white Polaroid photo! *No! Unfair!* "We need to head home right now!" I shouted. For there on that slick photograph with the scalloped edges was the image of a brand-new English Racer bicycle, sitting in the basement of our home back in Boulder!

I knew that soon we would head to Fort Worth to spend the rest of our Christmas vacation with our relatives on Mom's side of the family. That was the opposite direction from Boulder. It would be a whole week before I could ride that bike! The Polaroid picture dished out the worst kind of punishment—delayed gratification. It was far and away the best present I'd ever received. But here was the rub; I hadn't received it yet. I only knew of its existence.

Dad sensed my dilemma. "Gary, we couldn't fit it into the trunk of the car," he explained. "Mom and I discussed not telling you until we got back home, but then we thought the anticipation of what was waiting for you would be better than not knowing."

You thought wrong, Dad! Where am I supposed to put this disappointment so that it doesn't ruin the rest of the trip? It was then that I first learned what

A DAUGHTER'S WISH

The idea for an instant, develop-in-a-minute Polaroid camera was born in an era when instant gratification of this type simply wasn't possible. Edwin Land's three-year-old daughter wanted to see the photos her daddy had just taken of her right away. That wasn't possible in 1943. It would take Land five long years of delayed gratification to be able to satisfy his daughter's wish.

By 1972 nearly 20 percent of the five billion photos taken by amateurs each year were Polaroid prints. And by 1987 one out of every ten homes had a "Land" Polaroid camera.[44]

delayed gratification meant. I have no idea what words Dad used. I only remember that he thought the wait would sweeten my eventual enjoyment of the bike and that understanding delayed gratification was part of growing up.

I still remember seeing my English Racer for the first time there in the corner of the basement and riding it for hours all bundled up against the cold. I enjoyed that bike for many years, exploring and stretching the horizons of my world atop those one-and-a-quarter-inch tires. It was only when I decided to turn it into a unicycle (which you cannot do with an English Racer) that it finally found its way to the dump.

I had no idea how important the mastery of delayed gratification would be. It prepared me to wait for the right woman to marry, gain the endurance needed to get a Ph.D., and face the serial disappointments of getting a book into print. You were right, Dad. There is a deep satisfaction found in the anticipation of something a long time coming.

WHAT MY DAD TAUGHT ME

In a world of instant gratification, one's stomach may be stuffed, but one's soul is seldom sweetened in the rush.

> *When I was a boy of fourteen, my father was
> so ignorant I could hardly stand to have
> the old man around. But when I got to be
> twenty-one, I was astonished at how much
> the old man had learned in seven years.*
>
> —Mark Twain

My First Dog

Ever notice that your head and heart can be complete strangers—that you can think one thing and feel the opposite? I know things in my head that, at times, I find impossible to get my heart to accept. For instance, I am quite certain that a benevolent Creator, who has my best interests at heart, governs life. Yet fear can grip my heart and tell me that I'm on my own and ill prepared for the future. It's silly I know, but knowing alone won't mend the fractured relationship between the thinking part of me and my feelings.

Go too far down this road, and society labels you schizophrenic. Pretend that the war between your head and heart doesn't touch you, and society says you're in denial. We're all cut off from our true selves to some extent. This crack in our psyches stems from weeds that took root in the Garden of Eden—lies about the Father-heart of God—and they continue to sow themselves into open and untreated wounds of the soul. I keep a list of these heart-lies in the back of my Bible. Some seldom touch me at all. One in particular is an old nemesis with more wins than losses. Our battle began on the day the world ceased to be a safe place.

For six years Waddles and I were inseparable—a boy and his dog. I can still remember the wonder of watching her with her one and only litter of pups, teaching her to jump through a Hula Hoop, racing across the fields near our house, and curling up with her next to a warm fire on a snowy night. The wag of her tail and her sharp bark always welcomed me home—until one day in the spring of my twelfth year.

The last days of school were dragging by, and summer beckoned as I walked from the bus to the front door. Dad was there to meet me. "I've got something hard we need to talk about," he said. "Waddles died this afternoon. She was playing next door, and our neighbor accidentally backed over her with his car." He enfolded me in his giant arms, and we cried.

Dad had already prepared a small wooden box and dug a grave under one of the apple trees in the backyard. Together we placed Waddles in the ground, filled in the grave, and started to deal with the hole in our hearts.

I don't remember the exact words we shared that afternoon. But I do remember bits and pieces of the wisdom my father spoke as he helped me to place death in its proper context. "Everything we have is on loan from God," he said. "Tears are an important part of life. Don't

COMING TO TERMS WITH GRIEF

Grief is a natural reaction to loss, but unresolved grief can last a lifetime. Significant loss weakens our ability to trust, detaches us from our feelings, leads us into isolation, and leaves us with a sense of abandonment. Grief recovery is a process that one cannot do alone.

Theresa Rando views the process of grief as a progressive move from recognition to reinvestment. Here are the steps she advocates:

1. Recognize the loss (overcoming shock and denial).

2. Confront the loss.

3. React to the loss. (Make the loss real to the mourner's experience.)

4. Recollect and reexperience the deceased and the relationship (a necessary mental and emotional reorganization often found through telling their story).

5. Relinquish the old attachments to the deceased (letting go of what has been lost).

6. Accommodate the loss.

7. Readjust and move adaptively into the new world without forgetting the old.

8. Reinvest. (Be willing to risk again.)[45]

bury your heart in the grave of someone you love."

In a lifetime of father/son talks, that was the single best conversation we ever had. Little did we know that six months later, I'd be standing at another graveside—my dad's, trying to say good-bye the way he taught me. Only this time, I didn't have a daddy to walk me through the hurt. The one who always interpreted life and its accompanying scrapes and bruises was gone. As a result, my head and heart went their separate ways, split by the heart-lie that God was utterly faithful and gracious—up to a point.

The world wasn't safe any longer because there was no one I could really count on.

It was such a diabolical lie. No amount of evidence to the contrary could pry loose the "feeling" that someday God's providential care would simply run out. Better not trust your heart to Someone who could one day walk away. Better lock it up and keep it safe.

Of course I didn't *think* I'd done such a foolish thing. I actually thought I had come through Dad's death pretty much intact. In fact, I don't think I shed a single tear during the next five years. I was the "man of the house" now. I was out of touch with my feelings and out of touch with being out of touch.

Oh, Dad, I lost my childhood when I lost you. I stayed lost a very long time. You warned me that my head and my heart could become strangers—that no one could ever really live in their head. But that's exactly what I tried to do.

WHAT MY DAD TAUGHT ME

No matter how great the pain, killing your heart only makes it worse.

> *Blessed are those who mourn,*
> *for they shall be comforted.*
>
> —Matthew 5:4

FOLLOW THE THREAD

ong before my first visit to the world of Jim White, I was well acquainted with his story. My dad had filled my head with Jim's adventures, explorations, and near-death experiences. Dad's first visit to Jim's world profoundly marked him as a boy. He became a student of this historical mentor and passed along each lesson to me. It was only a matter of time before he would introduce me to that world in person.

Seems Jim was riding the New Mexico range when he saw a dark cloud moving with a mind of its own across the open morning sky. At first Jim thought it must be smoke from a fire. It turned out to be thousands upon thousands of bats returning home after a night of feeding. Jim followed them home and discovered the entrance to an incredible underground world—Carlsbad Caverns.

Armed with some food and a lantern, he ventured past the twilight opening and into an uncharted world of bottomless pits, cold-wet darkness, and miles of mazes. At one point, he fell into a pool of water, dousing his lantern. In the total blackness, he took his lamp apart, dried it off, and finally got it lighted again.

Jim knew that the twists and turns of that underground world could disorient him within a dozen steps. So he tied one end of a piece of twine to the entrance and the other end to himself, playing it out as he went. No matter how disoriented he became, all he had to do was follow the thread back to the surface and home.

During one of his numerous trips below the surface, he stumbled across the skeleton of an earlier explorer—an Indian who'd lost his way. I still remember the day Dad pointed out where the Indian's body had been found during our exploration of the caverns. "Lose your grip on the thread or select one that breaks, and you, too, may find yourself wandering in the dark," he said. "Hang on to the thread, and you're as good as home."

Of course, there's more than one kind of thread. The lessons from Jim White transcend spelunking and spill over into how we navigate our own stories. Too bad most of us never bothered to tie one end of our narrative thread to home before we ventured into the uncharted territories of life. It's easy to lose one's way, become disoriented, and end up lost.

PRODROMOS

The ancient Greek mariners often found themselves holding both ends of the rope in a storm. The coast of Greece is lined with plenty of safe harbors; the problem is that storm-beaten rocks block most of them. Try to navigate a ship past these obstacles during a storm, or even during calm weather, and the sharp rocks will likely gut the hull and send you to the bottom. So what do you do?

Some sailor figured out that what a clumsy, slow-turning ship couldn't navigate, a small, nimble rowboat could. He lowered the smaller boat (called a *prodromos)* into the water after tying one end of a rope to it. Then he climbed in and used the smaller boat to steer past the rocks and into the harbor, trailing the rope behind it. Once in the harbor, the prodromos end of the rope was secured to the dock. Now all the sailors on the ship had to do was pull in the rope and the ship would slip past the rocks into the deep harbor along the path taken by the prodromos.

If you ever find yourself in need of a prodromos, you may want to take a long look at Hebrews 6:20: "Jesus has entered [the veil] as a prodromos (forerunner) for us." That's the only time the Bible uses that word. Once was probably enough.[46]

Dad saw to it that I was well-grounded—knew where I fit in the story. As the first grandson, not only was I a "gift from God," I was "G. L. Stanley III." I could trace my Christian faith back five generations. Life was not an accident or a cruel joke. It had purpose and a final destination.

That's not to say I didn't lose my way for a season. When Dad died, I fell into a deep pool that extinguished my thirteen-year-old heart. It took a long time to rekindle my doused flame. But when that light was restored, I was able to pick up the narrative thread that had been carefully attached to my life by my father, and I could follow it back home.

Carlsbad Caverns isn't really on the way to anywhere. You'll probably never just stumble across it; you have to make it your destination. I explored that cave in my late twenties after recovering from extensive knee surgery. I was just learning to walk again. I arrived before dawn to watch the massive gathering of bats returning from a night of feeding (just like Jim had watched a lifetime before). I left my crutches in the car and took my first long walk in months through the caves. Those early morning hours when I was practically alone with the stalagmites and stalactites were a holy time.

The guides no longer sing "Rock of Ages" during the normal tours. Instead, they fill their visitors' ears with geological theories as to how and when it was all formed. Sad. I wonder when they lost their grip on the thread that would have led them back to the Creator who fashioned it with an artist's eye and a lover's heart as one of His hidden cathedrals?

What My Dad Taught Me

Explore all you like, but don't let go of the rope.

> *Our Father refreshes us on the journey*
> *with some pleasant inns, but will not*
> *encourage us to mistake them for home.*
>
> —*Stacy Rhinehart*

REMEMBER THE ALAMO

On Sunday, March 6, 1836, the 13th day of the siege, 189 men failed to hold the walls of their small mission fort. After repulsing the first two attempts, the opposing force of some 1,400 Mexican troops, led by Santa Anna, successfully stormed the walls. For the next one to five hours (no one knows for sure) the fighting went from room to room. A half-dozen wounded survivors were taken prisoner, only to be summarily executed a short time later. Though only a footnote in the vast scope of human history, it was a defining moment in the lives of the men involved.

It didn't take the participants by surprise. It wasn't thrust upon them. They *chose* to take a stand at the Alamo. They knew what was at stake. It was not an abstract concept. These men had faced the concrete realities of life and death before. They knew they were outnumbered ten to one. They knew there would be no prisoners taken. They knew the hope of reinforcements was slim to none. They knew. They had a lot of time to think about it. They could have stepped aside. They didn't. Here was something worth dying for—and they did.

I was five or six years old when Dad thought we ought to visit the old mission that stands as a monument to the likes of William Travis, Davy Crockett, and Jim Bowie. Later when I learned to read, Dad supplied me with a series of biographies of great Americans—from Benjamin Franklin to, well, Davy Crockett.

In the movies, everything looks bigger. The inside of an airplane seems big enough to turn a tank around in. When I saw a movie of the Alamo, it looked roughly the size of the Astrodome. When I saw what was left of the real thing, I was surprised to see how small it was. It was dark inside—holy. That heroic moment in time took place in something closer to the size of a stable than a sports palace.

That day, Dad bought me a coonskin cap (complete with tail), a toy rifle, and an almost genuine Indian beaded belt, and I joined the ranks of those who fought Santa Anna for Texas independence right alongside John Wayne. On another day, I might be Zorro, Superman, or Hiawatha, but in that moment, I possessed a young boy's heart, eager to leap into the fray and lay down my life for this good cause.

Daddy had a similar heart, only his was a man's heart rooted in reality. The Alamo is real. And that is a big chunk of the difference between a boy's courage and a man's courage—one is abstract and costs little, the other is concrete and may cost everything.

I wish I could remember a specific time when I saw Daddy's bravery displayed, a time when he stood up to some punks hassling a little old couple, a moment when the gentle giant unpacked a bit of the power stored in his big body.

Dad was a Golden Gloves Champion (I think he had two or three fights all totaled, so it wasn't a big deal). But he did teach me how to box when the neighborhood bully had it in for me. He didn't seem all that interested in personally dealing with the bane of my life for me. I thought Dad might march over there and straighten out my sworn enemy. Instead, he held the notion that I ought to learn to fight my own battles—at least the smaller ones. So he made a punching bag out of an old olive-green canvas duffel bag filled with paint cans wrapped in an old mattress and hung it from one of the joists in the basement. He bought me some boxing gloves and became my sparring partner. He taught me about leverage, how to throw my weight into a punch, how to take a punch, block the other guy's swing, step inside, and land one of my own.

I never had to fight the neighborhood bully. Perhaps my willingness to "have a go" put a new perspective on the whole thing as far as he was concerned. Still, I can't recall a single time when Dad ever came close to using his skills as a fighter—not with his fists anyway.

I do remember heroic times when he stood up for a cause as the lone voice of opposition. I saw him face personal disappointment and financial ruin with a calm trust that ran deeper than the circumstances.

When Dad came to Colorado, his dream was to build a frontier village above Estes Park. He formed Ute Enterprises, negotiated land, gathered financial backers, and formed alliances with Trailways Bus Lines and the Stanley Hotel. We even went to Disneyland to see how to do it. But a local banker fled to the Caribbean with millions of dollars of other people's money and crashed the local economy.

Dad's dream died. His backers, many of them good friends, lost their money. Agreements and timetables ran out, and failure knocked on our door. What did Dad do? He started over. I don't recall him ever criticizing anyone behind their back or complaining that life was unfair. He knew that failure doesn't have the final word and that no mere man could control his life or destiny.

There was one time when I saw my father in a physical fight. We'd been tossing a football around the night before, but the next morning when he woke up, he couldn't move. An ambulance came and took him to Denver University Hospital. "Guillain-Barre," the doctors called it—a disease of unknown origin that attacks the nervous system. All he could move were his eyelids. They put him in an iron lung.

Guillain-Barre was survivable, but his case was extremely severe. Mom and I visited him every day and talked to a face that couldn't even smile. Dad continued to blink his eyelids, and after several days we figured out that he was trying to communicate with us that way. I suspect he remembered Morse code from his days as a Boy Scout. But we didn't.

Mom worked out a crude code where he blinked at the correct letter as she recited the alphabet and each word was spelled out. It was a frustratingly slow process. But the first thing he spelled was something to the effect that God was still in control and always had been. Then Dad spelled out a hospital joke he'd been thinking about.

Over the next few months, he began to make small but encouraging improvements. The doctors took him out of the iron lung for short periods each day to strengthen his ability to breathe on his own. I still remember when he was finally able to slowly move his fingers and briefly lift a single tissue, the sweat pouring down his face. He never gave up. How could he when he knew full well that there was Another with him in the iron lung who had already conquered death?

The Alamo is a monument to how a

SANTA ANNA'S ULTIMATE DOWNFALL

Santa Anna is best known as the general who lost Texas by winning the Alamo. Though he outnumbered the 187 defenders of the Alamo better than ten to one, he lost more than six hundred men in the attempt. Two months later, at the Battle of San Jacinto, it took him only eighteen minutes to lose to a force half his size. Santa Anna's career continued its ups and downs. On eleven occasions he won and subsequently lost the presidency of Mexico. But his ultimate downfall wasn't due to his checkered military career; it was his *sale* of New Mexico and Arizona to the United States seventeen years later that permanently removed him from power.[47]

group of men died. They came to that place to die for something bigger than themselves. After holding out for twenty-seven days, they were overrun by Santa Anna and his army. But history would later show that they won in defeat, for the Alamo was the turning point in the fight for independence.

Life's challenges seldom translate into a physical fight—though I suppose there are times when they do. Most of my challenges occur between my ears, and the fight is more internal than external. Remembering the Alamo reminds me of perhaps the most important lesson Dad ever taught me—you don't have to survive in order to win. Death isn't final, and there's more to life than just what happens between the cradle and the grave.

What My Dad Taught Me

Courage doesn't always win the day, but it never loses heart.

> *A successful performance at a moment of crisis rests largely and essentially upon the depths of a self wisely and rigorously prepared in the totality of its being—mind and body.*
>
> —Dallas Willard

YOU DON'T HAVE TO BE PERFECT FOR MY WORLD TO BE WHOLE

SECTION VI

MISTAKES AND MATURITY

It's difficult to let go of the illusion that your father was perfect, especially if he was a good dad as opposed to a neglectful, demanding, or abusive one. After reading a few stories about my dad, it would be easy to think that he was just about perfect. Or perhaps you suspect that I've succumbed to that desperate need in all children to see their father and their relationship with him idealistically.

I do have many more good memories than bad ones. Selective recall? Perhaps. Childhood idealization? Possibly. But I am aware of imperfections in my father. You have to sort out the good and the bad if you ever hope to meet your father as a real person. It is also an important part of growing up and finding the real you.

As Alden Nowland states in *Between Tears and Laughter*, "The day a child realizes that all adults are imperfect, he becomes an adolescent; the day he forgives them, he becomes an adult; the day he forgives himself he becomes wise."

KiNG TUT'S SPiDER-RETRACTiONS AND CORRECTiONS

on't you wish life were like a newspaper? If you got the facts wrong, made a mistake, or let a deadline dictate your morals, you could just print a retraction somewhere in the back of the paper and everything would be set straight. Well, I have a retraction of my own to make. Come to think of it, life *is* like a newspaper, only instead of retractions, we make confessions. Confessions are better than retractions. One sets the record straight; the other sets us straight. I'll take forgiveness over correction every time.

It all began with a poetry assignment in the fourth grade. I think my teacher was reading epitaphs to us from the Spoon River Anthology. In any case, I went home in need of an idea and some direction for my writing project. Dad was more than helpful.

I'm pretty sure Dad came up with the idea for the poem and "nudged" the crafting of it. Pretty sure his help is what elevated "our" poem into the local newspaper. What an accomplishment!

Looking back on my first published piece, I have some mixed feelings about it, getting credit for something I didn't exactly do by myself. Actually, I cheated, if you want to take the poem out into the light and take a close look. I suspect I could let my mind wander and come up with other times when I cut corners, worked the system, and took the easy way out.

Recently I went back through the Boulder Daily Camera morgue to see if I could find a copy of "my" poem. I wondered if it was any good. Actually, I was hoping it was a real stinker so that I could believe I actually wrote the majority of it myself.

Hours of staring at microfiche in the public library netted me a headache, a nostalgic walk through Boulder in the 1950s, and no poem. Some things are better left buried. Perhaps that's why Dad didn't keep a copy of it in the family scrapbook.

It's not easy to allow your son or daughter to fail. But failing that, there is a greater danger of leaving them with an unacknowledged retraction in need of confession. Some lessons are a long time coming, unintended, and a bit sad because of the cost.

RESOLVING THE GOOD AND THE BAD

Part of growing up is learning to live with the reality that all people, including the best of fathers, are a mixture of good and bad, virtue and vice. Reconciling the ideal and the real isn't always easy. In Henry Cloud's book, *Changes That Heal,* he offers an inventory of questions to help you check your progress on resolving the good and bad in past, present, and future relationships. Here is a partial list:

PAST

Whose badness in the past did I deny? Have I seen it yet? Have I forgiven them?

Whose goodness did I deny? Do I still believe they are all bad? Have I forgiven them?

PRESENT

Which persons do I consider to be all good and deny their badness at present? Why?

Which persons do I see as all bad and deny their good parts? Why?

Who in the present have I not forgiven? Why?

FUTURE

Whose badness do I need to confront? When and how?

Whose goodness do I need to appreciate? How will I let them know?[8]

Luci is fond of saying that we all want to be associated with success. That is why we are prone to correcting our mates in public when they make a mistake. We don't want anybody to think that *we* married a jerk. No one wants their mate to look like a jerk—reflects badly on the spouse. The same holds true for parents and kids. We say we want them to make us proud when what we often mean is that we want them to feed our egos—make us look good.

If Dad had been a little less eager to feed me the words, perhaps I'd have learned a different lesson—what it really takes to make it into print and write beyond worn-out phrases and rhymes. It's one of few things I recall

Dad doing that reflects badly on him. He didn't need to do it. I knew my value didn't rest on a grade or in some teacher's perception of my work.

The irony is our poem on "King Tut's Spider," as I remember it, made a similar point. Tut's mummified body was little more than groceries and a housing project for our spider. No matter how lofty or hoity-toity you become, you always end up back at the bottom of the food chain—dust to dust, ashes to ashes.

WHAT MY DAD TAUGHT ME

It's fine to lend a helping hand, but don't carry the entire load if you're not supposed to.

Character is the real foundation
of all worthwhile success.

—*John Hays Hammond*

THE PETRIFIED LIE

The summer after I turned nine, we took the family vacation of a lifetime, visiting the Painted Desert, National Sand Dunes, Grand Canyon, Pacific Ocean, Disneyland, and the Petrified Forest. It was three weeks of motels, historic sites, long car rides, and a lifetime of memories.

We laughed and sang and ate out just about every meal—just the three of us. We climbed the sand dunes of southern Colorado (three steps forward, two steps back) and discovered that at the end of a run down a sand dune, the flat area hits you like a brick wall. We packed layers of colored sand in a Coke bottle from the Painted Desert. We discovered there's a 200-pound weight limit for riders who want to take a donkey down the Grand Canyon; Dad suggested he could switch donkeys along the way so as not to wear out the donkey. The guides didn't buy it, and we didn't go.

At Disneyland, we ascended to the top of the Matterhorn roller coaster, plumbed the depths on the submarine ride, laughed along with our jungle cruise guide, commandeered a canoe near Tom Sawyer's Island, and filmed it all on Dad's super-8 camera. I still have the films. It was the perfect vacation with only one small blemish—the Petrified Forest.

If you've ever been to the Petrified Forest, you remember the fossilized trees laying on their sides like prehistoric dinosaurs; the massive stone stumps begging to be climbed, and the cross sections of tree trunks with their rings numbered and labeled. There were also thousands of small bits of petrified wood scattered on the ground inside and outside the park.

A common piece of wood becomes a prized possession when it's petrified. I ran around collecting them like seashells on the seashore—a pocketful of pretty rocks was dumped on the floor of the backseat of the car. It was a great day . . . until we ran into a ranger post on our drive out of the park.

"Did you folks have a good time visiting our National Park?" asked the ranger.

"We sure did!" Dad replied.

"You know the preservation of our parks is a major concern," continued the ranger. "I have to ask, did you pick up any of the petrified wood for souvenirs? It is a criminal offense to desecrate a national park." His question let all the air out of our great day. Guilt crept into my soul.

Dad paused, then said, "We left the park pretty much the way we found it, sir."

The ranger smiled and we drove off with my ill-gotten souvenirs in a sea of silence. Mom said nothing. I said nothing. Dad said nothing. A mile or two down the rode, Dad pulled off to the side, got out, opened the back door, and we dumped my collection of petrified rubble on the side of the road.

SOME THINGS NEVER CHANGE

Tempting pieces of fossilized wood are still scattered across the Petrified Forest National Park, and it is still illegal to take any of it home. A ranger stationed at the exit to the park will still ask you about any unauthorized "souvenirs" you happen to pick up along the way. The park staff has encouraged the superstition that bad luck will come to anyone who steals these colorful little rocks, and every week finds another perpetrator returning his ill-gotten gain (sometimes taken decades ago). One other thing hasn't changed. Folks still help themselves to the forbidden rocks, removing several tons of them every year![49]

Dad didn't know it was illegal to let me collect those rocks until he was confronted by the ranger's question. In that moment, he had a choice to make. But it happened so quickly—came out of nowhere. At times like that, instinct takes over. The instinct for preserving his son won out over an honest confession. The ranger might have understood, but Dad didn't give him a chance to find out. Dumping the rocks didn't get rid of the guilt. Putting the rocks back wouldn't have put things right either. I could see it in his eyes.

I wish Dad had told the truth in the first place or gone back and confessed to the ranger in the second place. He didn't. I wish I could say I never had to repeat that lesson myself. I can't. We all get caught off guard. We all make mistakes in the heat of the moment. We are all eaten by the guilt of regret.

A few hours down the road, the incident wasn't as fresh and didn't worry me as much. But forty-one years later, I still remember that one petrified lie. I forgive you, Dad.

WHAT MY DAD TAUGHT ME

Life has a way of putting us in the position of either covering up or clearing up our mistakes.

Maturity is measured by the distance
between the sin and the confession.

—Gene Sealander

NEVER ON SUNDAY

I loved going to the movies as a kid, especially the Saturday morning flicks sponsored by the Watts Hardy Dairy. A "Francis the Talking Mule" film with Donald O'Connor or a classic western with either Roy Rogers or John Wayne was shone with a Looney Tunes cartoon and (usually) an episode from one of the old cliffhangers that used to populate the silver screen. Admission was two Watts Hardy milk cartons that were tossed into a big dump truck parked in front of the Boulder Theater. There was no sophisticated rating system back then—just movies.

One evening Dad decided to go to the movies by himself—not a date with Mom, not a family outing, just by himself. He said it wasn't the kind of movie I'd enjoy, and Mom didn't want to go—very odd. The movie he went to see was *Never on Sunday,* the story of a prostitute who had religious convictions that she shouldn't ply her trade on Sundays. It won an Academy Award. Today that movie could be shown in its entirety on television without raising a single eyebrow. But back then this romantic comedy was forbidden fruit—an adult film.

Dad never said much about his night out. There probably wasn't much he could say. It was such a minor incident. I only remember it because it was so uncharacteristic of Dad. But it opened a door I found all but impossible to close later in life. Tacit permission was granted by example.

A few years back I invited a friend named Ken to go to a guy's flick—an action movie. It was rated "R." He declined. When I asked why, he said he had three reasons—two sons and a daughter.

"Whatever I do," he said, "my kids will take a step further. If I don't

NEVER ON SUNDAY

Melina Mercouri played a prostitute in *Never on Sunday,* a Pygmalion story with an adult theme. Oddly enough, her romantic interest in the movie was her real life husband, Jules Dassin. The film was nominated for five Academy Awards and won the Oscar for best song. In 1960 there was no rating system, but today that particular adult comedy would likely receive nothing more than a PG rating. Mercouri is to be applauded for the good use she made of her fame as a movie actress to help her home country of Greece become a democracy, but there was a price. In its day, *Never on Sunday* was rather racy and controversial. The fact that it wouldn't raise a blush on most moviegoers today only goes to show how great the price has become.[50]

want them to fill their minds with the stuff in an R-rated movie, I'd better not go to anything rated worse than PG."

His comments were kind. Ken isn't the condemning type. But his words went deep—wisdom from a father's heart that applies even to his childless friend. For there are a host of witnesses who either cheer us on, weep over our poor choices, or follow in our footsteps. Often they go even further down the wrong path we've trailblazed for them. Unfortunately, I know. I went much further than my dad, and it took my other Daddy to bring me back.

WHAT MY DAD TAUGHT ME

You are always an example . . . even when you don't want to be.

> *How nice it would be if there were just something left these days that could honestly be called "unmentionable."*

A REFRiGERATOR ON THE FRiTZ AND HOW TO FiGHT FAIR

It was the evening before Thanksgiving. Thirty international students were to join us for a traditional holiday dinner the next day. We'd planned to catch a student play at the local high school, and in the meantime, I was relaxing by watching the evening news in the front bedroom.

"The refrigerator is making a strange sound," reported Luci, my bride of little more than a year.

"Hmm," I replied.

"Aren't you going to look at it?"

"Nope, I don't know a thing about refrigeration. A problem related to carpentry, electrical, or a bit of plumbing—I'm your guy. Refrigeration? Just be a waste of time, hon."

Luci left, and the news report continued.

Five minutes later, Luci returned, saying, "Do you know what's happening tomorrow?"

"Sure. We're having thirty international students over for Thanksgiving."

"Well, the refrigerator is starting to sound like it swallowed a demon, and all the food for tomorrow is packed inside it!"

I pointed out that it was after five o'clock and that I seriously doubted that there was a twenty-four-hour hotline for broken refrigerators. "Maybe the food will stay fresh since it's packed so tightly together," I offered.

Her frustration over my lack of willingness to own the problem with her, and my frustration over what I perceived as being asked to do what I couldn't, led to our first big fight as a married couple.

Voices were raised. Feelings were hurt. I threw our flashlight across the street and into the park. (It was the only time in my life I've ever thrown anything in anger.) Luci had never seen her dad raise his voice to her mom. So obviously she was married to a monster! I had never seen my dad raise his voice to my mom—I *was* a monster!

I stormed across the street, picked up my freshly bent flashlight, and returned to the kitchen. Still feeling very much put upon, I wrenched the refrigerator away from the wall and unscrewed everything I could find on the back of it. Dust bunnies flew, along with a number of unworthy thoughts.

As a kid, did you ever attach a playing card to your bicycle so that the wheel spokes hit it when you pedaled? Made a lot of noise, didn't it? Kind of like a motorcycle.

Well, on the bottom of just about every refrigerator, there's a barrel fan that cools the motor by pulling air through the front grill located under the door. Flopping around on the cooling fan of our refrigerator was a blue paper napkin that had been sucked into the fan. It was making as much noise as any playing card flopping on a bicycle's spokes.

You have no idea how unfair it was that I could *actually fix* the blasted thing! The absurdity of the moment released the tension, forgiveness was sought and given, and we discovered a big hole in our upbringing. Our parents never modeled for us how to fight fair. Dad always said, "Your grandmother used to say, 'The key to a good marriage is never to go to bed angry—even if you have to stay up all night.'" Well, that's a nice sentiment as far as it goes, but how do you do it?

Until the evening of the refrigerator incident, I'd thought it was a good thing that I'd never seen my parents fight or have a serious disagreement. I was wrong. Resolving conflict in marriage is a critical skill my dad neglected to teach me. Perhaps Mom and Dad worked through their problems behind closed doors. Perhaps they just stuffed their disappointments with each other and hoped that time would heal the wounds. It doesn't—not really. Mask? Cover up? Bury? Most certainly. But healing takes more than time. It takes loving confrontation, courage, and compassion to

THE THIRD OPTION

Peacemaker Ministries promotes six biblical ways to respond to conflict.

1. **Overlook it.** There are times when the best course of action is to deal with the wrong you've suffered in your own heart and silently forgive the other person. (See Proverbs 19:11.)

2. **Discuss it.** When the wrong should not be "overlooked," loving confrontation between the two of you may resolve the problem (confession/forgiveness). (See Matthew 18:15.)

3. **Negotiate it.** Sometimes the best option is to compromise and seek a win/win solution. (See Philippians 2:4.)

4. **Mediate it.** When discussion or negotiation breaks down, get outside help to work through the problem. (See Matthew 18:16.)

5. **Arbitrate it.** When a voluntary agreement cannot be reached, agree to binding arbitration before those who can fairly hear both sides and who will also seek the best for both of you through reconciliation. (See 1 Corinthians 6:1.)

6. **Discipline it.** If steps one through five don't work, and the obstinate person claims to be a Christian, bring the problem before church leaders in hopes of bringing about justice, repentance, forgiveness, and reconciliation. (See Matthew 18:17.)[51]

forgive, let go, and seek help.

Dad died young, so the long-term effects of what he modeled are harder to see. But they are there. I talked with Mom the other day and asked her to forgive me for some specific things.

"There's nothing to forgive," she said.

"Sure there is," I replied. "I've hurt you and failed to see my own neglect of my one remaining parent." She still has a hard time taking old hurts out, talking about them, and giving them to our Heavenly Father for healing. The wait-and-see method may calm today's storm, but it won't ever change the weather patterns of a relationship.

I wish I'd grown up seeing something different—something that taught me how to deal with my own marital conflict rather than just pretending it never happened or throwing a flashlight into a dark park. Fortunately, the lessons don't stop when you leave home, and my other Daddy knows all about modeling loving confrontation.

WHAT MY DAD TAUGHT ME

Not everything my dad did or didn't do is worth emulating.

> *Time doesn't heal—healthy time in the light heals. Buried wounds just fester.*
>
> —Henry Cloud

WHEN HUMANS MARRY

"I don't want your parents' marriage," Luci said to me one day.

Hello! Where did that come from? What makes you think it's even true? And what's wrong with the way my folks lived out their marriage anyway?

"This is *our* marriage, not theirs," my wife continued, obviously much further down this particular road than I.

It set me to thinking about the way Dad treated Mom. He loved her. I still remember the stories of how he'd travel miles and miles to her North Texas home only to find her gone. Lovesick, he didn't stray from his pursuit of Myrtle McGowen. In the end, he won her; neither of them was yet twenty-one when they married.

I also remember the story of how they eloped. When they returned to Dad's parents' home the next day, he didn't have the nerve to tell Mammuddy and Pop Pop that they were married. What a blow to a fledgling marriage! His folks knew they'd been together overnight, and Dad let the suspicion of indiscretion linger for nearly twenty-four hours—not the kind of thing any bride would cherish. Mom decided to let him linger in his own stew until he owned up to what he'd done.

What were you thinking, Dad? Wish I'd known the story while you were still here so that I could have asked.

I also remember stories of how they embraced life's adventures together as a young couple—trying to incubate chicken eggs under the bed and all of the eggs going bad, their willingness to try a myriad of jobs from Mom's days as a dance teacher to Dad's stint as a politician.

All of my cousins loved to spend time with Uncle G. L. and Aunt Myrtle. Life was exciting around them. They both lit up the room as well as those in it. They liked each other.

But there was the time when Dad was engaging every stranger in the restaurant and ignoring Mom. "Why is it that you can talk to everyone else and can't carry on a conversation with your wife?" she asked him.

It reminds me of the time when I was being uncharacteristically cute and witty in a conversation with Luci when she asked, "Are you trying to talk with me, or are you performing for the strangers around us?" I was performing.

UNWRITTEN FAMILY RULES

It should come as no surprise that we bring into our marriages conscious and unconscious patterns of relating that we internalized in our families of origin. Setting aside those patterns, good or bad, as *the* way to relate is part of what is meant when God says, "For this cause a man shall leave his father and his mother" (Genesis 2:24).

One practical way of recognizing those unwritten family rules and what to do about them is for each of you to write down your version and compare notes. Unwritten rules usually sound like the following:

- "We always buy the generic brand."

- "We never inconvenience anyone."

- "We don't share our problems outside the family."

- "We are the responsible ones and thus we can never be dependent on others."

You will probably need some time and prayer to surface your own unwritten family rules, but as you do, talk them out with each other and see how each one squares with God's written family rules. He doesn't have that many, and He frequently sums them all up in one or two verses. Oh yes, He's not in to "unwritten" family rules in His home.[52]

Dad was the dreamer, and Mom was the practical one. Dad was self-employed and enjoyed the uncertainties and inventiveness that went with it. Mom taught school like her mother. Her job gave us the security of a steady income and medical insurance. His job infused life with the wonder of what lay over the next horizon. She kept us well-grounded. He taught us how to fly.

It's easy to look back now and see that Dad let Mom carry too much of the burden. He needed less security than she did, and so she lived on a hook that he had little experience with. But he was also the one who hugged away her cares and carried her beyond the safety of a less colorful world. I'm more like Mom when it comes to living on the hook. I'm more like Dad when it comes to living with inconsistency. How in the world did I manage that? There's a lot about being a husband I didn't learn from my dad.

How did you romance Mom in the everyday parts of life, Dad? I saw all kinds of love between the two of you, but little romantic love. Oh, you were more in touch with your heart, but how did you lead in the mysterious dance of masculinity and femininity? I didn't see enough of the steps to become proficient.

Yes, Luci, this is our marriage and not my folks'. Forgive me for not realizing it sooner and finding other resources to fill in the gaps that are inevitably left out by even the best of fathers.

WHAT MY DAD TAUGHT ME

We each enter marriage with a picture in mind of how it's supposed to be; tear up the picture before it tears up the marriage.

Falling in love is easy; growing in love must be worked at with determination as well as imagination.

—Lesley Barfoot

YOU DON'T HAVE TO BE RELIGIOUS TO ENJOY GOD

SECTION VII

REAL HOLINESS

What is the first image that comes to your mind when you're asked to picture a "holy person"? Take a moment and try to form a mental picture of holiness. If you're like most of us, you conjure up images of scented candles, a crèche, somber music, and definitely no smiles. Holy evokes images of someone who is straight-laced, sober, and sad—someone who's not much fun.

Who would you say was the epitome of holiness or the holiest person who ever lived? Jesus? Jesus was way holy. But how does your definition of holy square with how you see Jesus? Jesus was a party-goer. His followers were accused of not conforming to the general notion of holiness (Matthew 9:10-17). Jesus said things that were funny (Matthew 7:3), got mad (Matthew 21:12), hung out with "sinners and tax collectors" (Luke 7:34), and didn't keep the rules (Mark 2:23). Jesus was a major scandal to those in the pious religious crowd. He had too much fun; folks felt at ease around Him (Luke 10:39 or John 13:25). Jesus wasn't what you normally think of as religious. He was *real.*[53]

The goal of life isn't to become more religious. It's to become more like Jesus. What a relief! I think my dad got it, as you'll see in the stories that follow.

THE ENTIRE BOOK OF ADHESIONS

very family has some bit of shtick that is regularly dusted off and celebrated. Like an old piece of music, it conjures up pleasant memories of other times and places. Words are mouthed and smiles anticipate familiar refrains well in advance of each spoken slice of nonsense.

I can't count the times Dad pulled out the well-creased pages of his one and only sermon and held forth at a church fellowship dinner or living-room gathering. We have no idea where it actually came from. Mom is still quite sure that G. L. wrote the whole thing. However, I've run across enough variations of his sermon to conclude that Dad added his two bits to an oral tradition he embraced somewhere along the way.

I've heard somewhere that the average prostitute in eighteenth-century London knew more of the Bible than the average churchgoer does today . . . wouldn't surprise me if it were true. Still, it's amazing how many of the familiar phrases and images that season our everyday conversations are based on some biblical passage or story.

I suspect some might find Dad's sermon a bit too irreverent (probably better off just to skip over it and save yourself the aggravation). However, for those willing to subject their biblical literacy to some clever (and corny) play on words, subtle ironies, and the humor that populates the Book of books, read on. For laughter is the sound of Heaven, not the clucking of tongues.

Howdy bruthern and sistern. I've been an evangelist since I was four. I found my first sermon to be the most relevant and materialistic message found in our convention today. Due to the universal appeal of the Scriptures, I have not varied one tot or tittle from my original message.

Some people say that religion is for the unedjucated and suspicious. But I tell you, even from my humble background, I had no trouble committing the parables and teachings to memory. You recall that in the Book of Maccabees, verse 46, we see clearly that our standard is the little child and my mind has continued to hold that standard for the last thirty-eight years! And I will continue to maintain this pure, undiluted message for as long as I fill the pulpit.

And now, this evening if you will all open your Bibles to the thirty-third chapter of the book of Adhesions, we will begin.

And lo, the Queen o' Sheba gathered together her share of her father's wealth and set off for a far country, and she spent her money in sightless living until she was flat broke and she found herself living among the hogs. And a fire come down out of heaven and the flame did lick up the water from the trenches, the sacrifice on the altar . . . the very altar itself, and baked all them hogs and it was hard to separate the husks from the ham but she did eat till she could eat no more.

And then she stood and said, "I am unclean." So she went down to the river and washed the spittle from her eyes three times, and when she saw clearly from afar off, she said, "I will arise and go unto my father's house. And she rode a day's journey asittin' on a young mule when the mule flung her off and she fell among thieves. Five was wise and five was foolish. And she did hide herself under a bushel and passed by on the other side.

And as she wandered about forty years in the desert she saw a great light and heard a voice calling, "Sheba, Sheba!" And she replied, "Here am I Lord, send me!" And the sea parted and she did run into a cloud about the size of a mustard seed. And some fell on good ground and some on bad and stony ground. And the whole earth was flooded forty days and forty nights. And the animals cast lots to see who to throw overboard. The Good Samaritan wins the toss and elects to throw her overboard. While in the water, she was swallowed up by a large fish. At the end of three days and three nights, the fish spit her up and she did walk across on dry ground.

She continues down the road and sees a man atearin' down his barns to build bigger ones. She attempts to buy some food with thirty pieces of silver, and the rich young ruler tells her to go and hang herself. She climbs a pine tree, 'cause she is short of stature, and casts her net on the other side. And she seed a ladder running up and down with My Shack, Your Shack, and a Bungalow, the famous real estate agents, singing, "Great am Susanna, the Queen of Sheba."

Off in the distance she sees the leaven tower of Babel. Standin' on the balcony is Jezebel in her bathrobe of many colors. And the Queen of Sheba set her face to the

A HUMOROUS TWIST

During the eighteenth century, no skeptic delighted in finding humor at the expense of the Bible (and Christianity in general) more than Francois-Marie Arouet, better known as Voltaire.

His rejection of a personal God— of God as Father—is undoubtedly linked to the rejection of his own father. His confusion over his own lineage (he thought himself the illegitimate son of Rochebrune) and quarrels with his father led him to repudiate his father's name in favor of the pen name Voltaire.

Voltaire's running feud with the Bible led him to proclaim that within a hundred years, the Bible and Christianity would be virtually extinct and pass into history. It is more than humorous that a mere fifty years after his death, the Geneva Bible Society had made Voltaire's house their headquarters and were printing and distributing Bibles from there.[54]

East and did walk around the walls seven times and did toot her horn. And a mighty voice from a nearby burning bush called, "Fling her out!" And they flung her out, seventy times seven. And there was a wailing and a snatching out of teeth and that old Jezebel she busted into so many pieces that they couldn't be counted for the multitude thereof. And they gathered up twelve basketsful, five loaves, and two fishes before the cock crowed thrice.

Now the question I asks you dearly beloved brethren is, in the Judgment, whose wife am Jezebel agoin' to be?

If you will all turn to hymn twenty-two, we will sing the benediction.

What a mess! When life's story is a jumbled patchwork of episodes and fractured notions, the answers to the questions we ask at the end of the day aren't going to be worth much. Like a wise man once told me, "There is no right answer to a wrong question." And a hymn tacked on to the end won't sort it out.

WHAT MY DAD TAUGHT ME

It's important to get the facts straight, but you don't have to be stuffy about it.

> *Most people are bothered by those passages of Scripture they do not understand, but the passages that bother me are those I do understand.*
>
> —Mark Twain

THE PLIGHT OF LOT

Dad was a thespian at heart. He loved to perform and make folks laugh. I still have his box of old magic tricks. His fingers were too thick for much close-up magic, but he could be counted on to show any lingering tot how his thumb came apart at the joint and stretched to twice its normal length. Mostly he loved to amuse anyone who'd sit still with his linking rings, restoring rope trick, and magic milk pitcher. Magic is 90 percent verbal, and verbal was Dad's forte.

Our family performed elaborate puppet shows at Building Trade Exhibitions and PTA fund-raisers. The Junior Jaycees, the Lion's Club, and Elks Club all provided a stage for Dad's antics. At least once every year or so at a church fellowship dinner, Dad played Lot and his obstinate wife (both roles!) in a madcap dialogue on the eve of the destruction of Sodom and Gomorrah.

Dad's only prop for this fanciful farce was a billed cap. He wore the bill forward when he played Lot and reversed it when he became Lot's wife. Lot was a bundle of nervous energy, jumping up and down as he delivered each line. Lot's wife had a high nasal voice guaranteed to get under your skin as she constantly fussed with her hair.

As the story progressed, Dad's changes of character became more complex, and part of the humor was Dad's confusion over which part he was playing and which way his hat was turned. As the couple made their escape from Sodom, Dad delivered Lot's lines while reaching back with his hand to drag his reluctant wife along and said Lot's wife's lines with his arm extended in front as if being pulled along. Here's a faithful rendering of his performance. And now, ladies and gentlemen, I proudly present *The Plight of Lot:*[55]

Lot: Come on, woman, we have got to get out of here before it's too late!

Wife: We can't go yet, there's a sale on tomorrow, and I want to buy a new bracelet to go with my sandals.

Lot: Didn't you hear those two angels! The whole place is going to be destroyed.

Wife: Don't get pushy with me, Lot. You were the one who insisted on coming here in the first place.

Lot: Who cares? The thing is, we've got to hurry!

Wife: Well, at least take time to finish your goat's milk. You know how hard it is to get good goat's milk, and I'm not going to throw it out.

Lot: Okay, okay, anything, only let's go!

Wife: Now where did I put my makeup bag? I can't go anywhere without that.

Lot: Come on! I'll get you a new one.

Wife: I've heard that one before. Besides, think what effect this is going to have on our children.

Lot: I am.

Wife: This is their home. What about their friends? Sneaking out of town like this. Everyone's going to think we've done something shameful.

Lot: Shameful? In this town! We're leaving NOW!

Wife: I don't know where you got all this energy all of a sudden. You're as lazy as a camel when it comes to doing a little work around the house.

Lot: Oh, LORD, how long! [time passes] Finally, just a little faster, and remember, don't look back.

Wife: What a lot of nonsense! My mother always said you were a bum.

Lot: Right, I'm a bum, only just keep moving.

Wife: Did you remember to lock the front door?

Lot: In a couple of minutes there won't even be a front door. Forget all that and remember not to look back.

Wife: We just have to go back. I think I left the stove on.

Lot: The stove?

Wife: Can't we rest a little while? Why couldn't we leave at a decent hour?

Lot: By morning, Sodom and Gomorrah will be nothing more than ashes.

Wife: I told you we should have turned off the stove.

Lot: *(Mumble)*

Wife: What was that?

Lot: Nothing. Forget it.

Wife: Don't look back. What a lot of nonsense! Oh, what a pretty sunrise!

Lot: Never mind that. Why did you stop? Wife? Wife?

[Lot tugs and pulls, afraid to look back to discover why his wife has stopped. Then he wets his fingers, reaches back, and touches his wife, and then he pulls has hand back, licks his fingers (tasting

---

THE COTTON PATCH GOSPEL

One of the most imaginative and entertaining versions of Jesus' life is set in the Deep South—Valdosta, Georgia. Old truths are wrapped in new words and bluegrass music that is likely to get past the defenses of pew sitters and scoffers alike.

In this world, "Man does not live by grits alone," and "it's easier to squeeze a hog through a knothole than it is for a rich man to enter the kingdom of heaven." You've never heard Harry Chapin's music if you haven't heard his version of the Hallelujah Chorus," called "Jubilation."

Tom Key and Russel Treyz wrote the book, and Harry Chapin wrote the music. I've watched the video at least thirty times. Look for it in your local Christian bookstore or find it on line.[56]

the salt) and groans. Finally, he shakes his head and trudges off stage without ever looking back.]

Dad brought the Bible to life and taught me through his antics that it wasn't some old book stuffed with stale stories that had nothing to do with me. These were real people, and if you looked at them with fresh eyes, you could find a lot worth taking home that you might otherwise miss. I've spent much of my life teaching folks the same thing.

WHAT MY DAD TAUGHT ME

There's nothing boring about the Bible, but there are sure a lot of folks doing their best to make it seem so.

> *He will yet fill your mouth with*
> *laughter and your lips with shouting.*
>
> —*Job 8:21*

iT'S EASiER To SAY Good-BYE AND LEAVE

i never tire of visiting the subdivisions Dad built. Homes that were once on the outskirts of town have somehow found their way into the middle of communities. Twig-like trees I watered as a boy now block most of the sky; yards I leveled with our little double-clutch tractor are now terraced flowerbeds.

None of the families who live behind those walls ever met the man who designed and built them. I doubt they'd be remotely impressed that the boy who tiled their bathrooms, picked up scrap lumber in their yards, and watered their seedlings was standing out front some thirty-five years later.

Perhaps my ability to mentally see through the outer walls and run down the houses' hallways causes me to drive a bit slower when I pass through neighborhoods. One house in particular draws me back. Though I've driven by it many times, I've never stopped and knocked on the door. It's the kind of house you would see in *Better Homes and Gardens.* I still have the newspaper clippings extolling the innovations and unusual design of that house in Edgecliff. It had a stockade fence that surrounded acres of lawn and a good-sized pond. It was the only home we ever had that could accommodate a menagerie of animals from Weimaraners to Tennessee walkers, and from geese to donkeys.

Its gabled ceiling and open floor plan provided a spacious environment for lots of people. The flagstone fireplace and circular staircase with a banana tree in the middle set it apart as something special. If ever there was a party house, this was it. Some of my best memories occurred during the year we lived there. It was the place where I learned to ride a bicycle, lost the keys to the subdivision, learned to make allowances, and encountered scorpions for the first time. But it is also the place where I first tasted loneliness.

I don't remember the occasion; perhaps it was a Christmas party, for the season was brisk and everyone arrived wearing a coat. Friends and family began to arrive shortly after dark. Each ring of the doorbell promised our home would soon be full of family and friends. There were kids to play with and room in which to run. The food was delicious, and the laughter filling.

Mom was the perfect hostess, and Dad made everyone feel right at home. The crackle of the fireplace invited everyone to shed their coats as well as their cares. We had a wonderful time. But the hour grew late, and while some of our guests helped clean up, others began to gather their coats and say their good-byes. Mom, Dad, and I escorted each one of them to the front door and waved them home.

THE HEART'S DEEPEST DESIRE

Every heart shouts that there must be more to life. Our deepest satisfaction is always incomplete. We can deny it, sate it with lesser things, bury it and hope it won't bother us any longer, or we can follow it back to its true source.

It first surfaced in my life as loneliness when I was five years old. I have since found that heart longing to be a recurring theme in the writings of my favorite authors.

C. S. Lewis called it the "inconsolable longing." Pascal reportedly called it "a God-shaped vacuum." Augustine called it a "restless heart." G. K. Chesterton called it our "divine discontent." Gerald May calls this desire the "awakened heart." John Eldredge calls it our "heart's deepest secret." I call it "having to say good-bye and stay."

With the departure of each family, the house grew quieter and somehow emptier than it had been before they came. All too soon it was just the three of us in this big house. No doubt Mom and Dad had worked all day preparing for that party. They were tired, but it was a good tired that required little comment and no hint of regret. But in that moment, I experienced something new— something sad and lingering—I felt lonely *in Dad's presence*. It was as if each good-bye had taken a bit of me with it, and I was no longer whole—no longer content with what I was or had been before. I learned that night that it is easier to say good-bye and leave than it is to say good-bye and stay.

I was only five years old at the time. I had no place to put my loneliness. I couldn't name it. I couldn't even put it into the question, "Why wasn't Daddy enough?" I know now that the answer to my loneliness didn't lie within the walls of that house. It never did. It didn't even lie within the man. I know now that I had a longing much more profound than anyone, or for that matter any number of human beings, could fill. I know now that I was made for something more—another party in a far grander home with another Host who won't just make me feel right at home, I will be home.

Perhaps it was the convergence of these truths that night that awakened in me that longing I couldn't name. I can name it now; it is a reminder that I have an open invitation to step into God's presence right now. We all do . . . because He misses us too.

WHAT MY DAD TAUGHT ME
My dad will never meet all of my needs; he was never intended to.

> *God has been calling us home to His arms,*
> *where we belong, since the Garden.*
> —*Sandra D. Wilson*

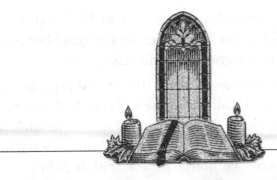

THE DAY THE EARTH DIDN'T MOVE

I watched Dad wear out three Bibles. I listened to him pray. I touched his tears as he wept over the pain of sin in someone else's life. God was a part of his daily life, and he wasn't bashful about sharing the Good News with others. But faith was more than a personal commitment or private practice. Faith was played out in community.

My folks taught Sunday school classes, led various church committees, volunteered to do visitation, and tithed. They answered my questions, took me to church, and made sure that I was enfolded in and around the family of God. I was in church nine months before I was born.

Dad and Mom were also concerned that I develop a faith of my own and not merely hitchhike along on their faith. Faith wasn't an obligation or duty; neither was it a foregone conclusion. Faith was an open invitation.

Every Sunday we sat in church, and every Sunday I heard an invitation to "walk the aisle" and receive Christ. And every week I just sat there. I knew the facts: God loved me; Jesus died for me; He rose from the dead; and I was a sinner and needed to receive Him as my Savior. But how do you know? How do you know it's your time?

I developed a strategy for finding out. I decided I needed a sign. So I told God that I would walk the aisle and invite Him into my life as soon as He arranged a small earthquake during the invitational hymn. Perhaps if I'd lived in California, this might have worked out, but I lived in Colorado where the earth never moved. After a while I figured that another sign might work just as well. If God would just cause the lights to go out during the hymn, I'd know He wanted me to give myself to Him. The electricity never failed. Finally I said, "If just three people go forward on the second to the last verse of the final hymn, I'll be the fourth one down the aisle." Never happened. So there I sat right next to my Dad.

The summer of my ninth year, I went to church camp near the Garden of the Gods. I got the top bunk, and our pastor, Brother E. J. Speegle, took the bottom bunk in our tiny cabin.

After the activities of the first day, as we were settling in for the night, E. J. asked me what I thought about camp and church. I'm not sure how our conversation happened into the area of my "pew sitting" during the weekly invitations, but it did.

I explained my earthquake strategy, my power outage strategy, and the bit about three folks walking the aisle on a particular verse. He listened to it all and smiled.

"Gary," E. J. said, "I understand your need for a miracle to confirm your decision to give your whole life to God. Only makes sense. What do you think about the business of Jesus rising from the dead after three days in the grave?"

Well, I had no trouble believing that. That was the key to the whole thing! If that didn't happen, none of it was true.

"Don't you think God would want you to put your trust in *that* miracle rather than something like a timely earthquake, a flickering light, or someone else's decision?" he concluded.

When he put it that way, I saw that I already had all the evidence I needed to walk the aisle. In fact, that night I found a faith of my own as Brother E. J. led me into the Father's forgiving embrace. The next Sunday, I was on my way down the aisle on the first verse to let everyone know that I had asked Jesus into my life.

Where was Dad during the most important decision of my life? Why wasn't he the one to encourage my second birth rather than E. J.? I think he knew his presence would overwhelm my ability to make my own choice. So he did what was likely the hardest thing he had ever done—he stayed in the background and entrusted me to the Daddy of us all. No one was more proud. No one grinned any wider than my dad on the day I walked the aisle. A lifetime of prayers and planting produced a harvest in the soul of one son.

Dad only saw the beginning stages of my new life. But I found E. J. in Wolf, Texas, decades later. His wife, Ruth, had died a few years before, and he lived near his daughter and son-in-law. E. J. didn't want to live with them because he wanted to be available for any other "pew sitters" in the nursing home that might need a bit more assistance in preparing for their next life.

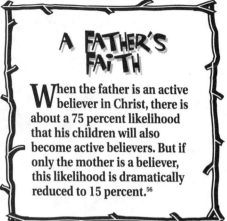

A FATHER'S FAITH

When the father is an active believer in Christ, there is about a 75 percent likelihood that his children will also become active believers. But if only the mother is a believer, this likelihood is dramatically reduced to 15 percent.[56]

Luci and I walked up to him as he was talking to a couple of elderly skeptics, and I said, "Hi, I'm Gary Stanley from Boulder, Colorado. Do you remember me?"

His eyes crinkled for a moment, and then he said, "You're Myrtle and G. L.'s boy!"

He was eager to hear what had happened as a result of that night near the Garden of the Gods. I told him everything I had longed to tell my dad, and his eyes moistened as he listened. Hours later, his words washed over me, affirming my life and completing the circle. It was the last benediction I ever heard from his lips: "I'm sure your mom and dad are very proud of you, Gary."

WHAT MY DAD TAUGHT ME

Everyone has to find a faith of his own. A dad's job is to help his children find the right one.

There's always enough evidence for those
willing to believe; there's never enough
evidence for those who refuse to believe.

YOU'RE NOT A GREAT MAN

Some conversations stick. Small talk that takes an unexpected turn leads you down a path you've never considered before. In that moment, you are changed beyond your imagining. Sometimes it is a careless word by a friend that mortally wounds a relationship (like, "You can do better than her."). Sometimes it is a word carefully planted that finds hungry soil ready to nurture the seed into something beautiful. Words spoken over us can have profound consequences.

Madeline Harris has known me most of my life. Her middle son is my age; our families went to the same church. We were in each other's homes. We were in each other's lives. She watched me grow under the tutelage of my dad and recognized the remarkable man that he was. She happened to be married to a remarkable man herself.

When Dad got sick, the Harrises and Joneses and Etheridges and Rogers and others rallied around Mom and me. After Dad died, those same families became surrogate brothers and sisters and moms and dads to me.

What do you say to a fatherless child? How do you help him find a place for the wounding? How do you help him make the transition from boy to man when his natural model is gone? Perhaps you just love him, let him hang out at your table, play with your kids, look for signs of the father in the boy . . . and pray.

I have no memory of anything particular that Madeline ever said or did during the years our families' lives were intertwined. I ate her food, roughed and tumbled with her son, and thought it strange that her kids snacked on fruit when clearly a "snack" has to be something sticky, sweet, and synthetic. But beyond that, she touched my life no more or less than the other church families of my adolescence—until years later.

The Harris family moved to Colorado Springs, and our families no longer crossed paths during the ordinary course of life. We occasionally ran into each other at retreats and kept in touch through Christmas cards and letters, but had little other contact until I was twenty-seven.

I was at the front end of raising support to be a missionary. I quickly discovered I wasn't very good at it. Every time I picked up the phone to call a potential supporter, I developed a serious back problem that took the form of a large yellow streak running up and down my spine. Finally, I decided that I needed some help and encouragement.

That's when I thought of Madeline's husband, Harlan, who was the pastor of a large church in Colorado Springs. The Harrises put me up and allowed me to speak to their church members. I was brilliant, engaging, and humble, but I didn't raise so much as a penny. However, I left that place far richer than when I arrived, all because of a handful of words spoken to me.

After Madeline cooked and served us breakfast, Harlan left for church. I was packed and ready to drive back to Boulder. The trip had been a waste of time. I wondered if I'd ever make it to the mission field. Madeline sat across from me at the breakfast table sipping her coffee. She didn't look any different then than she did when I was just a kid.

"Gary, there's something I've wanted to say to you for a long time," she said.

"Yes, Madeline, and what might that be?"

"You're not a great man."

"Thanks, Madeline, I appreciate the candor."

"Oh, hush and listen! You're not a great man yet. I don't know if you ever will be. But you possess one of the essential ingredients for greatness. Your father was one of the most remarkable men I've ever met, and you lost him at one of the most vulnerable seasons in your life. God has allowed you to be wounded as deeply as any wound can go. It is a wound you will carry the rest of your life. If you're willing, it can become the place where God has immediate access to your heart. I think He may lay you open through that wound if you let Him—and letting Him has always been the key to greatness."

With those words, Madeline marked my life. The growth of the seed she planted still goes on. I don't think I ever told her. She is a wordsmith herself with several books "under her pen." She tends to write biographies of great men. I never thought of the connection between her words to me and her choice of subjects until just now.

Ah, Madeline. Thank you for helping me to see how a severe wounding can be a loving invitation. I'm still at the front end of

WHAT TO DO WITH WOUNDS

Being wounded is a universal experience. Our wounding leads us to question and doubt, crying out, "God, where were You? You could have prevented this! Why didn't You?"

My wife, Luci, and I have a friend whom we will call "Laura." Laura was the victim of deep childhood wounding. One day she asked God again, "Where were You?" and He answered, not audibly, but no less clearly, "Every time you prayed, I heard. Every time you wept, I wept. There's no way that you with your finite mind can understand fully why I gave human beings the power to choose either good or evil." And then He asked Laura a question: "Do you trust Me?" She has learned that she trusts God to the degree that she believes He unconditionally loves her.

What do you do with wounds? Take them to your Heavenly Father. "His (God's) boundaries around my enemy haven't been the boundaries I would have chosen," Laura has written. "I would have shortened the chain around the neck of the roaring lion. But I know Him (God) well enough to know that with great thought, with great care, with great love He chained the roaring lion and measured the length of his chain."[58]

this thing, but oh, how right you were. God's favorite door is surely a wound.

WHAT MY DAD TAUGHT ME

A great start isn't worth much if you don't finish well.

The quickest way to the heart is through a wound.

—John Piper

time you need look no further than your relationship with your mom to find its origins. But I couldn't see it. Mom wasn't domineering, didn't try to get all of her emotional needs met through her only son, and wasn't overly protective. She let me grow up. After Dad's death, she seemed to embrace life and move on. It didn't make sense.

During the break, I explained to the speaker that although I had started to recognize my own anger towards women, I couldn't trace the root of it back to my mom in any overt way. He wisely responded, "I can't really tell you what's going on in your situation. However, we do have a scheduled time of prayer coming up. Why not ask God for some clarity during that time?"

Talk to God? This was a workshop on prayer counseling, but I hadn't been thinking about its applicability to me. I decided to

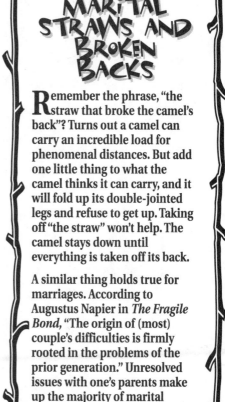

MARITAL STRAWS AND BROKEN BACKS

Remember the phrase, "the straw that broke the camel's back"? Turns out a camel can carry an incredible load for phenomenal distances. But add one little thing to what the camel thinks it can carry, and it will fold up its double-jointed legs and refuse to get up. Taking off "the straw" won't help. The camel stays down until everything is taken off its back.

A similar thing holds true for marriages. According to Augustus Napier in *The Fragile Bond*, "The origin of (most) couple's difficulties is firmly rooted in the problems of the prior generation." Unresolved issues with one's parents make up the majority of marital burdens. The issues between spouses are usually "the straw."[59]

pray. I had no idea just how much my life was about to change. It is changing still.

WHAT MY DAD TAUGHT ME

At the heart of every issue we face is a relationship.

> *If you're not willing to face the real you,*
> *you'll never know who you really are.*
>
> —Sandra Wilson

DON'T SAY
IT'S ALL RIGHT
IF IT ISN'T

As I faced the anger toward women that I had discovered, I bowed my head and prayed, "Father God, where does this anger come from? Help me. I don't want to be an angry man." I'm not sure what I thought would happen.

I found Him answering my prayer by leading my thoughts back over the significant events of my life. Soon I arrived at the day my daddy died. Much of my life hinges on that singular event. But then I was reminded of what happened the evening before. . . .

Dad had spent four months in an iron lung, paralyzed by the little-known disease, Guillain-Barre. Mom took a leave of absence from teaching, rented a small basement apartment near the hospital, and did all the things nurses can't do. She cared for her mate.

Aunt Judy and Uncle Fred came up from Texas to stay with me. My life flitted back and forth from our home in Boulder to a Denver hospital, from eighth-grade classes to major life lessons, from the safety of an intact family to a world of uncertainty.

The Guillain-Barre had left Dad completely paralyzed, but he was still able to feel all of the discomfort that goes with most hospital stays. Since he could be given nothing stronger than aspirin to ease his pain, it was hard for Dad to sleep. The intravenous needles, the inevitable collapsing veins, the constant noise of the machine, and nurses coming in and out all conspired to keep him exhausted. We were all exhausted. Our hope was in God and the fact that others had recovered from this disease.

Then one night as we were about to leave the hospital, Mom said, "Do you want to say good-bye to your dad before you go home?"

I looked through the window of the door into his hospital room and said, "No, it's so hard for him to get to sleep. I don't want to wake him. I'll see him tomorrow."

Mom, who was worn down from months of hospital rooms, doctors, and hard choices, paused for just a moment and said, "All right, Gary. You go home now."

What she didn't say was that Daddy was slipping in and out of a coma. She didn't say that the doctors said he wouldn't live through the night. She didn't say there would never be another chance to say good-bye.

I didn't know it at the time and wouldn't make the connection for nearly thirty-five years, but her decision not to tell me and my response to that decision would leave me stuck and unresolved in heart and spirit for decades.

The next day I was in the backyard where my first dog, Waddles, was buried. I was hunting imaginary big game with my bow and arrow when Aunt Judy and Uncle Fred came out of the house, hugged me, and said, "Gary, your daddy died last night."

It seems everyone knew it was coming but me. The most important news in the world came too late for me to do anything about it.

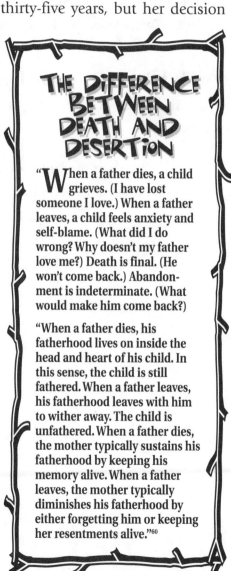

THE DIFFERENCE BETWEEN DEATH AND DESERTION

"When a father dies, a child grieves. (I have lost someone I love.) When a father leaves, a child feels anxiety and self-blame. (What did I do wrong? Why doesn't my father love me?) Death is final. (He won't come back.) Abandonment is indeterminate. (What would make him come back?)

"When a father dies, his fatherhood lives on inside the head and heart of his child. In this sense, the child is still fathered. When a father leaves, his fatherhood leaves with him to wither away. The child is unfathered. When a father dies, the mother typically sustains his fatherhood by keeping his memory alive. When a father leaves, the mother typically diminishes his fatherhood by either forgetting him or keeping her resentments alive."[60]

Mom was wrong in not letting me face Dad's death in that moment. However, she did a wonderful job of keeping his memory alive after Dad was gone. I was wrong in letting that decision clog up my heart to the father love that was always available from the Father of fathers.

WHAT MY DAD TAUGHT ME

You can't hide from your problems; they will seek you out.

> *A father of the fatherless and a judge for*
> *the widows, is God in His holy habitation.*
>
> *—Psalm 68:5*

THE HOSPITAL VISIT

While the workshop on prayer counseling moved into a discussion of "presenting issues" and the "anatomy of anger," my heart and mind returned to the hospital room where I last saw Dad. For the next hour and a half, I relived the details of Dad's last four months on earth. Now understand, I have always been aware of these events; I didn't block them from my memory. I just had never fully realized what the experiences did to me. But God did, and in the safety of His presence, I was able to understand more than I ever had before.

I will always remember the configuration of the hospital room. Dad's iron lung was along the left-hand wall; the two beds in the ward were at right angles to Dad and had modesty curtains. The institutional tile floor, the smell of antiseptic, the sound of the iron lung pumping, the less pleasant hospital smells, the constant movement of hospital staff, snatches of conversations overheard from visitors to the other patients all flooded back.

And Dad. His lips were usually caked with dry yellow spittle that had to be wiped off. The rubberized fitting over the opening in his throat distorted the sound of air coming in and out of his neck . . . the smell of bad breath . . . his tired steel-gray eyes . . . the window on the side of the iron lung and the towel that covered his waist . . . the intravenous lines. His arms and legs were covered with purple bruises where veins had collapsed from "cut downs"—the only way to find a deeper vein to pump fluids into him. I recalled his bout with jaundice when his skin turned a sick yellow, and the day I put my finger over the hole in his throat so that the air went through his mouth and he could talk in short sentences. His withered body was like something out of a concentration camp.

He was so helpless—completely paralyzed. Totally dependent for every little thing. I remembered the day Mom angled a mirror above his head so that he could see something besides the ceiling.

GUILLAIN-BARRÉ DISEASE

Guillain-Barré (pronounced "ghee-YAN bah-RAY") is now the most common form of sudden, generalized paralysis occurring in the Western Hemisphere. Experts still do not know how it is contracted (likely it is associated with antibodies produced during bacterial or viral illness that mistakenly attack the protective myelin sheath that insulates the peripheral nerves and spinal roots). One in one hundred thousand will come down with the disease; most will recover within a couple of weeks, although some take years, and 3 percent die.[61]

I remembered it all that day as I asked God about my anger. I was there as much as anyone can ever inhabit a memory. I wept the tears that had never come before. I sobbed out all the hurt stored up in a young boy's heart—all the hurt hidden deep in a man's soul.

In a way that I can't really wrap words around, I learned the biggest lesson of all that day from my dad. My life with him had been preparation for releasing me to the greatest love of all. When he died, I didn't know how to let him go. I was stuck like an arrow pulled back on a string. In that time of prayer, I finally said good-bye to my father, and it seemed like the bowstring was released and I was finally launched toward the Father-heart of God. Unstuck, I let the little boy out of my heart. It was time to grow up, forgive my mom, release my anger, and let God into that place only a daddy can inhabit.

It's a strange feeling to be older than the wisest man I ever knew and to know how little I still understand. I didn't realize it at the time, but the day I let the hurt out of my heart, I was one day older than my dad on the day he died. There are father-son connections that cannot be explained in the world of biology or social science.

WHAT MY DAD TAUGHT ME
I have another Daddy who will never leave me.

This is and has been the Father's work from the beginning—to bring us into the home of His heart. This is our destiny.

—George MacDonald

MARGiN NoTES AND DoG-EARRED FRiENDS

They say you can learn a lot about people by perusing their libraries. Some books are just for show—leather-bound classics with flawless bindings, unmarked pages, and gilded edges. Never opened gift books are kept out of some vague sense of guilt. Others are old college textbooks standing as silent sentinels to the struggles in acquiring knowledge now fragmented over time. Then there are the dog-eared, battered old friends that inhabit not only the bookshelf but also the owner.

Among my collection of books that once belonged to my father are family histories, a collection of poetry, and an odd assortment of titles ranging from financial planning to art. Two of them contain sections written by or about our family.

Frankie Wright Stanley (Mammuddy) and Alma McGowen Thompson were wordsmiths—a newspaperwoman and a teacher/poet. These grand progenitors crossed paths in my blood and in two books that I know of. One is a book of poetry from the women of the west Texas plains called "Pen Points," to which both of my grandmothers contributed several of their own poems.

The other is a book that chronicles the family histories of those who called Shamrock, Wheeler, and Childress, Texas, home after the Civil War. It is aptly titled, "Put Up or Shut Up."

I also have three worn Bibles that belonged to my dad. All are black covered. One is King James and two are the Revised Standard Version. Thumb through them, and you can learn something of their original reader. The corners expose the cardboard under the black leather. Pages are wrinkled from

A BIBLICAL DEIST!

A deist is one who thinks that "God created the universe and then moved away to let it run pretty much on its own." A "Bible deist" has substituted the study of the Bible for an intimate relationship with God. Few would ever want to own the label "Bible deist," but it is amazing how many of us have lived and been trained as if that were the ultimate goal.

Jack Deere wrote in his book, *Surprised by the Voice of God,* that "If the heart is the key, then the heart should get the most attention. But what we usually do in the church and in our theological schools is to assume that the heart is right, and then strive after the cultivation of the intellect. The process should be reversed."

a lifetime of sitting in the bathroom absorbing the steamy air of the shower.

My Bibles are underlined, color-coded, and full of notes from seminary classes and past sermons, memorable phrases, and outlines for books yet to be written. Open my dad's Bibles, and you will only find five small red marks in the margins. Dad lived in a time when you didn't write in your Bible. The King James wording brought out the poetry and rhythm of the text but often obscured the meaning behind ancient idioms and secondary meanings.

I wonder why Dad put those marks there. Was he simply marking his place in his daily readings, or was there something more significant behind them? Hard to say. He didn't mark the popular passages one learns in Sunday school. I have little written evidence as to how he spent his time in the Word. Guess he was one of those who'd rather live it out than write about it. I wish I were more like him. He never went to seminary, studied the original languages, or formally taught it to others. I have. But I've never worn out a Bible just by reading it over and over. My Bibles are worn, in large part, because I've studied them, parsed them, and lugged them around in a backpack.

I know far more about the outlines, origins, and organization of the Bible than my father ever did. But I think Dad had a heart-knowing of the Author that scholarship alone never finds.

WHAT MY DAD TAUGHT ME

God has never been interested in hiding behind His book.

> *You search the Scriptures, for you believe*
> *they give you eternal life. And the Scriptures*
> *point to me! Yet you won't come to me so*
> *that I can give you this life eternal!*
>
> —John 5:39-40 TLB

CRUISING FOR A PARKING SPACE

*P*icture this: Every person on the planet has the same idea you do—to visit the mall. The parking lot is full. You take a deep breath and join the motorized sharks on the cusp of a feeding frenzy. Eyes shifting back and forth for any backward movement suggesting a choice space about to open up, you jockey for position. You stake out a promising row. You follow shoppers loaded down with packages back to their cars.

It's not as if the lot is *entirely* full. The back lot, which is a three-day hike from the closest stores, has plenty of room. But you know deep in your soul that if you yield to the back lot and the long hike, you will eventually walk past a parking space right next to the entrance.

One of Mom and Dad's running arguments was whether or not it was appropriate to pray for a parking space. Mom was of the opinion that you shouldn't bother God with the trivial. Dad was of the opinion that God wasn't the least bit bothered by our asking for even the smallest thing. Mom would counter with the old conundrum that two competitors praying for the same thing puts God in the untenable position of playing favorites. Dad thought God was big enough to figure out a win-win for petitioners, even if he couldn't.

Dad prayed. Mom and I would watch to see if his prayer was answered. Not an easy thing to tell. We usually found a parking space in the general area Dad was praying in. But couldn't it all be coincidence? Did his prayer make any real difference? It became a running debate that seldom surfaced outside the car.

"Make prayer your first response, not your last resort," Dad would say. I imagine he was quoting some past preacher he had heard, but he'd made the truism his own. Mom and I were disposed to fret first and pray later. Our truism was, "Who says worry never helps? Most of the things I worry about never happen!"

At the least, Dad enjoyed the hunt for a parking space more than either of us did. He viewed life from a perspective I found hard to adopt, much to my regret. I remembered Dad's words a bit too late the other night when another truism reared its ugly head—"The devil is in the little things."

Another driver and I were waiting for the same parking spot—both of us with "rights." I'm sure we both wondered what the other would do. A family of four was taking their time getting into their car and out of "our" parking space. I'd followed this family to their spot in hopes of replacing their vehicle with mine. The other guy was simply waiting in their row for a parking space to open up.

There we both sat looking at each other through the windshield. He turned on his flasher, signaling his intention of taking the space. I sat and smiled, unsure what was best. There weren't any other parking spaces in sight. I'd "adopted" this family and their parking spot long before he even saw them. He was waiting in that row before I even knew this was their row. Life is never simple. I fretted.

PARKING FACTS IN AMERICA

- The total cost to provide parking spaces exceeds the total value of all the cars that use them.

- On average, every car needs four to five parking spaces (one at home and three or four elsewhere).

- For every 1,000 square feet of office space, four parking spaces need to be provided.

- On an average day, thirty-two different cars will occupy each parking space at an average fast-food restaurant.[62]

While I sat there, the other driver acted—he left! He smiled, waved a gracious defeat, and looked for another spot. I'd won! But when the family pulled out of the coveted parking space, I didn't feel like a winner. I felt like dirt.

Who did I think I was? Unfortunately, I knew exactly who I was. I was selfish, I was stubborn, and I was sorry I hadn't been the gracious one. I didn't like me very much.

Nor did I feel very festive when I walked away from my parked car. I was in need of forgiveness from a gracious stranger who had to walk a bit farther than I. I bet his step was lighter as the angels carried him along his "second mile." I know the demons that dogged my path made my short walk a marathon.

I seem to remember something about the first being last and the last being first. It's easy to forget when competing for a parking space. I don't really think we were put on this planet to compete with each other— there's plenty of space for the truly important. God is way too creative not to have figured out a win-win situation; we just need to ask Him what it is and trust what opens up.

I have a reserved space no one else can take, and God is always eager for me to fill it. Still, it has taken me years to realize that I'm not in competition for God's attention and love. Neither are you. There will always be a place next to His Daddy-heart, and He will never allow it to be filled with anything other than you. Bet you can find it if you ask. Bet it will remain empty for all eternity if you don't.

WHAT MY DAD TAUGHT ME

I never have to compete for a place next to Daddy's heart.

The only person you should ever compete with is yourself. You can't hope for a fairer match.

—Todd Ruthman

STANLEY HALL

The story is told of an ancient king who decreed that a monument be built in his honor that would stand for all time. On this monument, the king commanded that some eternal truth be engraved. What did the builders write? "This too shall pass away."

When a Roman hero returned from war, a parade was given in his honor. All the spoils of his conquest were part of the parade, and the populace lined the thoroughfare in his honor. However, riding with him in the chariot of honor was a slave who continually whispered in his ear, "All glory is fleeting."

I have my own reminder of this ancient truth. It is a simple plaque with "Stanley Hall" engraved on it. At one time that plaque hung in the fellowship hall of our church—a reminder of my dad's life and leadership in that community of believers. It hung there for years.

I still remember coming home from college one summer and finding it gone. Our church was two pastors further down the line. The membership had changed. Most of those who remembered and loved Dad had moved on. The plaque held no significance for those who frequented the hall. Those who embraced loving memories had attached it to the wall, but when those recollections had faded, little was left to hold the plaque there. So it was taken down without ceremony and stuck in a closet.

I felt the sting and hurt from Dad being forgotten. Unsure of what to say, I said nothing. Instead, I took the plaque home.

Thirty-five years later, I have my own collection of plaques and honors. All of them sit in a box in the garage. I have no idea what to do with them. At one point, I covered an out-of-the-way portion of my office wall with them—my "brag wall." Eventually, I took them down and in their place hung the tinfoil-covered cardboard plaque of the Duncan Yo-Yo contest I won when I beat out three other kids at the Table Mesa Shopping Center who showed up for the contest. Cynical? In my darker moments, yes. But mostly that cheap bit of cardboard reminds me of an even more ancient truth—don't take yourself too seriously.

WHAT EVER HAPPENED TO THE SEVEN WONDERS OF THE WORLD?

Few things manage to hold onto their place of honor over time. This holds true for six of the Seven Wonders of the Ancient World.

1) The Hanging Gardens of Babylon were built on the banks of the Euphrates River around 600 B.C. Until German archaeologist Robert Koldewey discovered some stone archways in 1899, there was little evidence other than a mound of muddy debris to suggest that the gardens ever existed.

2) The Statue of Zeus at Olympia was built around 450 B.C. In 200 B.C. the aging statue was restored. Eventually, some wealthy Greeks transported it to a palace in Constantinople where it was destroyed by fire in A.D. 462.

3) The Temple of Artemis was constructed in the city of Ephesus. Begun in 359 B.C., it took 120 years to construct and was destroyed by the Goths in A.D. 262.

4) The Mausoleum at Halicarnassus was constructed for King Maussollos, who died in 353 B.C. About all that remains is the word "mausoleum" and a few pieces in the British Museum.

5) The Colossus of Rhodes was a massive statue erected by the Greeks. The sculptor Chares completed it in 280 B.C. after laboring on it for twelve years. It was destroyed just a few years later in 244 B.C. by an earthquake.

6) The Lighthouse of Alexandria on the island of Pharos, built around 270 B.C. by the Ptolemies, stood nearly 400 feet high and guided sailors for 1,500 years. An earthquake destroyed the marble structure in 1375.

7) The Great Pyramids of Giza, built sometime in the millennium of 2,000 B.C. near the ancient city of Memphis in Egypt, is the only "wonder" of the ancient world to survive. They almost didn't. Napoleon's invading troops used the Sphinx for cannon practice. They shot off the nose but stopped when the red sandstone underneath caused them to fear it might be bleeding.[63]

It is a lie to think that you are more valuable if others notice you. It is equally untrue to think that the greater the number who honor you, the more important you are. It's easy to spend your life trying to be noticed. I know. I've tried. Everyone's "fifteen minutes of fame" is probably just fifteen minutes wasted. There is only one opinion that matters—God's.

Perhaps the folks at church did my dad a favor by taking down his plaque. I know they did one for his son. It's hard to take down a treasured memory and put it in the closet. But memories can get in the way of living, and if you don't move on, all that's left is stuck in a time warp. It's time to take the memory of Dad off the mantle of my life. It doesn't belong there. It needs to make room for something else.

WHAT MY DAD TAUGHT ME

There is One whose memory of you won't fade over time, or eternity.

The most important thing that parents can teach their children is how to get along without them.

—Frank A. Clark

DiRT-ROAD MEMORiES

After the prayer counseling conference, I knew I had more "heart work" to do. Some friends skilled in the ministry of intercession agreed to meet with me and help me along the way.

As we prayed, the eyes of my heart formed a picture of my dad and me walking up a hill. We were on a dirt road, side by side, on an adventure. We couldn't see what lay over the crest of the hill, but it didn't matter as long as we were together. The pace was easy, the load light, and the progress of each step satisfying. Then Dad stopped. It was clear he would go no farther with me. The prospect of going on alone was the saddest thing in the world. Fear settled in my stomach. I wasn't ready for this or whatever lay over the hill. I started to weep. I felt so lost and alone.

My friends interrupted my thoughts, asking me what I saw. I told them. The images and their implications seemed clear; I was mourning the loss of my dad and facing the sadness of life without him.

After a long pause, Russ, one of my praying companions, said, "Why don't you invite Jesus to give you more insight?"

What could Jesus do? Dad wasn't coming back. Still, I prayed and invited Jesus into the moment. In my mind's eye, He came striding confidently over the crest of the hill to meet us. When Jesus got to us, He hugged my daddy, and I steeled myself for their departure. But that's not what happened.

THE TRUE IMAGINATION

I am encouraged that writers like C. S. Lewis, Oswald Chambers, Dallas Willard, and Leanne Payne have all struggled to wrap words around what happens in times of prayer like the one I experienced. They all conclude that consciously engaging the eyes of the heart in our prayers is an essential part of knowing God's voice.

But how does one validate that the experience was something more than self-talk or wishful thinking? Leanne Payne writes, "The true imagination is engaged when we worshipfully listen in creaturely awe and obedience to God with our heart. Our heart receives pictures from the Lord."

"It is important to stress that the picture making faculty of the heart is not itself the true or higher imagination. Pictures are the language of the heart; like icons they are merely images through which the real shines. If the image is mistaken for the real, it becomes 'self-conscious' and thus a 'dumb idol.' The heart's capacity to image symbolically what it intuits is different from the intuition itself."[64]

Thou wilt keep him in perfect peace whose imagination is stayed of Thee.

—*Isaiah 26:3 RSV*

After greeting my dad, Jesus took Dad's place at my side. Daddy smiled and turned to take a different route. I looked up at Jesus, and He took my hand. He took Daddy's place—a place He'd only recently been invited into. He set an easy pace, and we continued the journey along the dirt road. We traveled much the way Dad and I had traveled to that point, the joy of each other's company overshadowing the uncertainty of what lay ahead.

I don't think God is limited in how He communicates with us. He could have taken me to a scripture that says He is a Father to the fatherless. He could have spoken through that still small voice and said, "Let your dad go and walk with Me into the next season of your life." But instead, He pictured that reality for me through the eyes of my heart, in the regions of the true imagination.

WHAT MY DAD TAUGHT ME

There are important things you can only know by heart.

I will never leave you nor forsake you.

—*Hebrews 13:5* NKJV

WHAT ARE YOU DOING WITH THOSE?

few months ago, Luci and I attended a conference on the Father-heart of God. The conference affirmed what God had been doing with the father issues in my life. The speaker spoke of his own journey and his roadblocks and breakthroughs in experiencing God as Daddy. He'd had a controlling, performance-oriented father who instilled in him the notion that he had to earn his way even though he could never quite measure up. I was tracking right along with him, listening perhaps more as an observer than as a learner. Luci, however, was using the opportunity to go deeper in her own healing process. When I informed her of how well I was doing, she asked, "Do you think you've come to the end of your father issues?"

Well, no. I suppose no one ever comes to the end of such a thing in this life. But I was pretty pleased with the progress I was experiencing. Still, her question troubled me. She often sees things in me that I don't.

I asked God if He had more He wanted to teach me, and immediately the image of the dirt road where I had pictured Jesus taking my father's place in the journey came back to me.

"What are you doing with those?" Jesus seemed to ask.

I looked to see what He was referring to and noticed that I was carrying a sack of rocks on my back and had more rocks stuffed in my pockets. I was even carrying a couple of rocks in my hands. Without really thinking

BUILDING ALTARS

Altars are an important concept in the Bible. Genesis records the building of seven altars, not counting stone pillars raised as memorials.

Noah built the first altar after setting foot on dry ground after the great flood. Abraham built three altars that reminded him of God's promise to make him a great nation. Isaac built one, and Jacob built two—all reminders of what God had done in and through them.

Altars were built as reminders that God is the one in charge and worthy of worship. They were meant to be instruments of worship. The same holds true today, whether the altar is made out of stone or memories put into a book.

Unfortunately, the seen is often easier to worship than the unseen, and many altars end up becoming the objects of worship rather than the means. When that happens, they become stumbling blocks that keep us from the very One who made the stones and gave us the memories in the first place. What are you doing with your altars?

I said, "These are the memories of my dad. I take them out and show them to folks from time to time."

He laughed and shook His head. "You aren't supposed to carry those things around! That's not what they are for! They were never meant to be a burden. I always hoped that you would use them to build an altar to Me."

I stood there in that moment and began to understand. "That's what this whole process is about, isn't it?" I asked, "Taking each memory of my dad, bringing it before my Heavenly Father, asking Him, "What do You see?" and letting Him show me how they all fit together—or how to trust Him with the ones that don't quite make sense yet.

You might want to try it for yourself. Take all the daddy stories sitting on your heart—the good ones and the bad ones—and look them over with the Daddy of daddies. Ask Him to help you understand how they were meant to fit together. Then build your own altar on the side of the road to the Daddy of daddies and set them down once and for all. I bet you'll be glad you did. I know I am.

WHAT MY DAD TAUGHT ME

Dads are to be loved, forgiven, and honored, but they're not to be worshipped.

> *Life must be lived forward, but it can only be understood backwards.*
> —Søren Kierkegaard

EPILOGUE

So where has all of this been leading? To the Father-heart of God. He misses you when you keep your distance. He longs for the kind of intimacy that allows you to become more of your true self in His presence. Every human father, good or bad, is meant to point his children back to the Daddy of daddies. God designed it that way. There is a father-hunger in each of us that can only be satisfied in Him.

My dad knew that. He was comfortable and comforted in God's presence. He regularly crawled up in His lap, rested in His embrace, brought Him all his hopes and dreams, fears and cares. I watched him do it in life, and I watched him do it in an iron lung.

I don't think Dad learned this from his father. Pop Pop was a good man, but I didn't see that kind of intimacy with God in his life. Perhaps Dad learned some of it from Little Red (my great-aunt Gertrude) or even his mother, my Mammuddy. But somewhere along the way, God became his Daddy, and that changed everything.

Having a great dad doesn't guarantee that God will ever be your Abba-Daddy. And having a not-so-great dad doesn't mean you'll never get that close to God. Dads point the way, but they can't take you there. That's a journey between you and the Father; you can only come through the Son. Jesus said, "I am the way, and the truth, and the life; no one comes to the Father but through Me" (John 14:6).

You may be hesitant to venture down this path because you're not sure about what kind of Father God is. Tell Him your concerns and fears. Ask Him to reveal His heart to you. That's what Philip, a disciple of Jesus, did. "Lord, show us the Father, and it is enough for us," Philip said in John 14:8. Jesus did just that; He showed him the Father. "He who has seen Me has seen the Father" (John14:9), He said. Jesus came to show us the Father and take us to Him. You can read more about it in the Gospel of John. Talking about His Father was one of Jesus' favorite subjects.

However, the journey to the Father ultimately leads to the Cross and the death of something near the core of each one of us—the hope of ever finding perfect father-love in another human being (even your dad). It is a matter of offering up those earthly relationships to God's healing and renewing touch. It is the prayer from a broken heart to the Heart of hearts.

Perhaps now would be a good time to go back and reread "The Other Daddy" on page sixty. I hope it will make more sense now. It took me thirty-five years to embrace the truth that I've always had a Daddy who was there for me.

ENDNOTES

1. Delthia Ricks, "Laughter really may be among the best medicines," (Orlando Sentinel) printed in *Health News*, Monday, November 4, 1996, p. 14; Brother Craig, "Health and Nutrition," *The Companion of St. Francis and St. Anthony Magazine.*

2. Josh Plass, "Moose" www.ticonderogak12.org/eighthgr/moose.html.

3. Interesting Facts cited in FunTrivia.com Homepage www.funtrivia.com/archive10.html.

4. Clifford W. Meyer, "The Candy That Saved the Marines," Copyright 2000 Tootsie Roll Industries, Inc. at Tootsie.com *Memories:* Veterans Remember.

5. Charles Downey, "Mortifying Moments," *Los Angeles Times Syndicate*, printed in *The Denver Post*, Wednesday, November 8, 2000, Section G, pp. 1,14.

6. Heidi Gabitzsch, "Samson the elk may have died at the hands of a poacher, but his death may have had a greater impact on Colorado wildlife than if he had lived to a ripe old age," *The Estes Park Trail Gazette*, Wednesday, January 17, 1996, Volume 27, Number 5; Jackie Hutchins, "Slayer of 'Samson' Enters Guilty Plea," *The Estes Park Trail Gazette*, July 17, 1996, Volume 27, Number 9; Tim Asbury, "Samson killer goes to jail," *The Estes Park Trail Gazette*, September 27, 1996; Tim Asbury, "Famed Trophy-sized Elk 1 of 4 Killed by Weekend Poachers," *The Estes Park Trail Gazette*, Wednesday, November 15, 1995, Volume 26, Number 43.

7. Mary Bellis, Inventors with Mary Bellis, "Footware & Shoes," http://inventors.about.com/mbiopage.htm.

8. "The life and times of America's greatest magician," www.magictricks.com/houdini/bio. htm.

9. Josh McDowell, *The New Evidence That Demands a Verdict*, (Nashville, TN: Thomas Nelson Publisher, 1999), p. 219; Hank Henagrath. bibleanswerman.com.

10. Mary MacVean, "Children's allowances can be tricky decision," *AP Special Features* (www.beloitdailynews.com/300/kids27.htm); Jeff Grabmeier, "Parents Hand Over $1 Billion to Teens Each Week," (www.newswise.com/articles/1999/12/ TEENCASH. OSU.htm).

11. Janet Hagberg, *Real Power: stages of personal power in organizations*, (Sheffield Publishers, 1984,1994); Janet Hagberg and Robert Guelich, *The Critical Journey: stages in the life of faith*, (Sheffield Publishers, 1989).

12. Pikes Peak Country Attractions Association, Copyright © 2000 by Pikes Peak Country Association and Electronic Storefronts, Inc., http://electricstores.com.

13. Mark 14:36; Luke 22:44; John 17:23; Romans 8:15-16; for more information see Tom Smail, *The Forgotten Father: Rediscovering the Heart of the Christian Gospel*, (London: Paternoster Press, 1996).

14   Sherrye Henry, "Keep Your Brain Fit for Life: What you should know, and what you can do," *Parade Magazine*, Sunday, March 17, 1996; "Your Memory - How to Improve It, Not Lose It" (Published - May 1999) isg.unicare.com/HealthyLiving/memory/htm.

15   "Water," *World Book Encyclopedia*, pp. 129-130.

16   John and Paula Sanford, *Waking the Slumbering Spirit*, (Arlington, TX: Clear Stream, Inc. Publishing, 1993), pp. 97-101.

17   Schlage's History of Locks "Keys from the Time of Nero to Queen Victoria" www.schlage.com/history/locks/locks01.htm - 10k.

18   J. Paul Caldwell, *Sleep*, (Willowdale, Ontario, Canada: Firefly Books, 1997), p. 188.

19   Medieval sourcebook: Salimbene: On Frederick II, 13th Century from the Chronicle of Salimbene, thirteenth-century Italian Franciscan, as translated and paraphrased by G. Coulton, http://www.fordham.edu/halsall/source/salimbene1.html.

20   Luke 6:40-42.

21   Fun Facts of Disneyland's Swiss Family Treehouse, "Swiss Family Treehouse Fun Facts," www.hiddenmickeys.org/Lost/DLSecrets/Tree.html - 10k.

22   Randy Marshall, notes from advanced communication class.

23   Studs Terkel, *Working: People Talk about What They Do All Day and How They Feel about What They Do* (New York: New Press, 1997).

24   tuckerclub.com; geocities.com; MotorCity/Garage/3166/autos/tucker.htm; teachingwithmovies.org.

25   Brad Knickerbocker, "The growing cost of gambling," *Christian Science Monitor*, Monday, June 7; David Snyder, "Counting the Cost of Gambling," CBN News, August 19, 1999; Valerie C. Lorenz, Ph.D, Robert M. Politzer, Sc.D., "Final Report of Task Force on Gambling Addiction in Maryland," Co-chairs Maryland Task Force on Gambling Addiction, 1990.

26   Edgar Rice Burroughs, *Tarzan of the Apes* (NY: Grosset & Dunlap, 1914), p. 1.

27   Shinichi Suzuki, founder of the Suzuki Violin Method also called the "Mother Tongue Method," cited in William and Constance Starr, "To Learn with Love," p. 125. Used with permission.

28   Sports History - Table Tennis, HickokSport.com, www.hickoksports.com/history/tablteen.shtml#olchamps.

29   *The Straight Story* starring Richard Farnsworth, Sissy Spacek, and Harry Dean Stanton. Directed by David Lynch. Written by John Roach & Mary Sweeney. Produced by Mary Sweeney & Neal Edelstein. Released by Disney.

30   Leos Ondra, "A New View of Mizar," leo.astronomy.cz/mizar/article.htm - 46k.

31   Thomas Dubay, *The Evidential Power of Beauty: Science and Theology Meet* (San Francisco: Ignatius Press, 1999), pp. 63-81.

[32] Brent Curtis and John Eldredge, *The Sacred Romance* (Nashville: Thomas Nelson Publishing, 1997), pp. 40-41.

[33] Janet Hagberg and Richard Leider, *The Inventureres: Excursions in Life and Career Renewal*, (Reading, MA: Perseus Books), tenth printing (1998), pp. ix, 12; and John Eldredge, *The Journey of Desire*, (Nashville: Thomas Nelson Publishers, 2000), pp. 153, 168,182.

[34] Jill Benford, "Bad news for motorists: Deer population exploding," at insure.com, www.insure.com/auto/deer.html.

[35] *Morrison and Fourmy's Ft. Worth (Tarrent County Texas) City Directory*, vol. 1936-1957, (Dallas: Morrison and Fourmy Directory Company Publishers); *Polk's Ft. Worth (Tarrent County Texas) City Directory*, Volume 1958-1974 (Dallas: R. L. Polk and Company Publishers).

[36] Curt P. Richter, "On the phenomenon of sudden death in animals and man," *Psychosomatic Medicine*, Volume 19, 1957, pp. 191-198.

[37] Shigeyuki Ito, "Smell and Memory," jacob@cardiff.ac.uk.

[38] Interesting Facts, www.geocities.com/Heartland/6741/interesting.html.

[39] University of Chicago's National Opinion Research Center, 1999.

[40] "TV Westerns - Hopalong Cassidy" "TV Westerns - Cisco Kid, Jim Bowie, Kit Carson" Corinth Films, Inc, corinthc@bellatlantic.net.

[41] Pro Football with James Adler, "Walter Payton Remembered" profootball.about.com/sports/profootball/library/weekly/aa110799.htm - 50k.

[42] Elisa Morgan, President of MOPS International (Mothers of Pre-Schoolers) which began in Boulder, Colorado.

[43] David Iler, "Colorado's fourteeners: Never lonely at the top," *Cyberwest Magazine*, September 24, 1995; www.geocities.com/wwwright/ColoradoSpeed.htm.

[44] Shoshana Ellis and Steve Jung, "Developed in a Minute: The Polaroid Land Camera," *San Juan Unified School District website*, October 29, 1997; www.sanjuan.edu/schools/arcade/PolaroidCameraJE.html - 16k.

[45] James John and Frank Cherry, *The Grief Recovery Handbook*. (New York: Harper and Row, 1988); Lawrenz Mel and Daniel Green, *Overcoming Grief and Trauma*. (Michigan: Baker Books, 1995) both cited in "A Grief Recovery Group" by Marsha Mills in an unpublished paper submitted for an MA class at Denver Seminary in 1997.

[46] A sermon by Truett Rogers in 1970.

[47] Lamont Wood, "Battle of the Alamo: Background," www.dmoz.org/Regional/North_America/United_States/Texas/Society_and_Culture/History/Alamo/.

[48] Henry Cloud, *Changes that Heal*, (Grand Rapids: Zondervan Publishing House, 1995).

[49] Arizona Guide - The Petrified Forest National Park - Conservation www.americansouthwest.net/arizona/petrified_forest/conservation.html 6k.

50 www.britannica.com/bcom/eb/article/2/0,5716,53402+1,00.html.

51 Peacemaker Ministries brochure adapted from Ken Sande, *The Peacemaker: A Biblical Guide to Resolving Personal Conflict*, (Michigan: Baker Books, 1997). For further information go to peace@mcn.net.

52 David Eckman, Acceptance: God's Change Agent for the Inner Life," from tape series *Acceptance and Gratitude*," tape number 1; see website kesed.com.

53 From a sermon by Phil Chorlin in 1999.

54 Paul C. Vitz, *Faith of the Fatherless*, (Dallas, TX: Spence Publishing Co.), pp. 14,38-39; John Ankerberg and John Weldon, *Ready with an Answer*, (Eugene, OR: Harvest House Publishers, 1997), pp. 333-334.

55 See Genesis 18:16.

56 Tom Key, Russel Treyz, and Harry Chapin, "The Cotton Patch Gospel," Bridgestone Multimedia, 1988; or order from www.store.dove.org/religious/cotton_patch.htm.

57 Keith Meyering, "The Small Group Letter," An interview in *Discipleship Journal*, Issue 49, 1989, 41 cited in *Tender Warrior* by Stu Weber.

58 "Laura," *The Chained Lion: A true story by "Laura,"* (Colorado Springs, CO: Lydia Press, 1999).

59 From one of many conversations with my uncle, John McGowen, who lived many years in Saudi Arabia.

60 David Blankenhorn, *Fatherless America: Confronting Our Most Urgent Social Problem*, (BasicBooks, A Division of HarperCollins Publishers, 1995), pp. 23-24.

61 Guillain-Barré Syndrome Introduction & Symptons/Causes & Treatment at http://onhealth.com/conditions/home/index,11.asp.

62 Donald C. Shoup, "The Trouble with Minimum Parking Requirements," Department of Urban Planning, School of Public Policy and Social Research, University of California, Los Angeles (UCLA), Los Angeles, California 90095-1656; see shoup@ucla.edu.

63 "Seven Wonders of the Ancient World," ce.eng.usf.edu/pharos/wonders/ - 6k.

64 Leanne Payne, *Listening Prayer*, (Grand Rapids, MI: Hamewith Books a division of Baker Books, 1994), pp. 156-162.

ABOUT THE AUTHOR

Gary Stanley was a Duncan yo-yo champion in the nine-year-old division of the Table Mesa Shopping Center in Boulder, Colorado. He still has the foil-covered cardboard plaque he won after beating out the other three kids who showed up. He can shell and eat more sunflower seeds in one minute than just about anyone on the planet and is a charter member of  The Plot and Blot Society (a writing group fashioned after the Inklings).

Gary also has degrees in psychology, theology, and a Ph.D. in Communication from the University of Southern California.

When Gary met his future wife, Luci, she was planning to be a single missionary in Japan. They haven't made it to Japan yet, but they have traveled throughout much of the former Soviet Union, speaking with the International School Project. They're also on the speaker team for Family Life Marriage Conferences. Gary is on the staff of Campus Crusade for Christ and is one of the founding faculty of the International School of Theology in Southern California where he taught for twenty years.

He authored *What My Dog Has Taught Me about Life: Meditations for Dog Lovers* and *The Garimus File: A Back Door Look at the New Testament.* He is also a contributing editor to the *Journey to Truth,* a member of the writing team for *Youth at the Crossroads,* and a contributing writer for *Christian Ethics and Morality: A Foundation for Society.*

Gary and Luci have no children of their own but enjoy an extended family with those God has brought into their lives. They now travel internationally, speaking and holding seminars on how to embrace God and life with your whole heart.